Praise for *Love the Narrow Path*

George Cargill, like a guide, leads us on a journey on the narrow God-love path. Weaving personal experiences and those of others with Scripture, Cargill points out those places on the path of joy and happiness, but also warnings that may cause us to stumble on our way. Regardless, God-love points the way on the narrow path so that we may proclaim, as Cargill writes, "Eureka! I have found it!"

—Sue Anne Lively, Professor Emeritus, Southern Nazarene University

Love the Narrow Path is an excellent daily devotional for all Christians who want a closer walk with God.

—Bernie Buckman, President of Buckman Wire & Cable, Deacon of the Roman Catholic Church

In this wonderful devotional, George Cargill shares insights for experiencing and extending God-love. What a joy to read an account of Christian love that is written so plainly, thoughtfully, and elegantly. Cargill's use of teaching moments, personal experiences, and historical examples throughout the devotional brings the devotional teachings to life. Readers will not only enjoy *Love the Narrow Path*, they will find themselves reflecting on the truths about God-love that it reveals long after they have finished the devotional.

—Rev. Jason A. Stevens, Pastor, Harvester Church of the Nazarene, St. Peters, Missouri

The simple wording of Cargill's reflection makes it available to a variety of readers at different places in their spiritual journey. Cargill takes a moment with each devotional to share an observation from his personal life that we can relate to. That shared experience draws us to the Scriptures and reveals a nugget of spiritual direction for our journey. With that aha moment, he leads us to prayer that we might commit our new insight to the Lord and to action.

The concluding prayer helps the reader not only remember the lesson and internalize it but lift up the heart yearnings as a prayer to God to step forward into the light that has been given. I recommend it for all of God's people on the journey of discipleship who are looking for daily words of encouragement.
—Rev. Joseph Purl, Pastor, Church of the Nazarene

George Cargill has done an excellent job of identifying crucial elements of living a life that follows the narrow path. Simple, yet not simplistic, daily devotionals that I would recommend for anyone, but especially new believers wanting to secure that their steps are on the right path.
—Stan Hall, Pastor, Gateway Church of the Nazarene

LOVE
THE NARROW
PATH

Let love rule !

George Cargill

LOVE

THE NARROW

PATH

Meditations on the Straight and Narrow

GEORGE CARGILL

NEW HOPE®
PUBLISHERS
Imprint of Iron Stream Media

An imprint of Iron Stream Media
Birmingham, Alabama

New Hope Publishers
100 Missionary Ridge
Birmingham, AL 35242
New Hope Publishers is an imprint of Iron Stream Media
NewHopePublishers.com
IronStreamMedia.com

Iron Stream Media serves its authors as they express their views, which may not express the views of the publisher. Portions of the articles included in this book may have been previously published. The profiles included are chosen solely by the author.

Library of Congress Control Number: 2021932249

Unless otherwise noted, Scripture quotations in the text of *Love the Narrow Path* are the author's own translation.

Scripture quotations marked (NASB) are taken from the New American Standard Bible®, Copyright © 1960, 1962, 1963, 1968, 1971, 1972, 1973, 1975, 1977, 1995 by The Lockman Foundation. Used by permission.

ISBN-13: 978-1-56309-426-2
Ebook ISBN: 978-1-56309-427-9

1 2 3 4 5—25 24 23 22 21

Dedication

To my mother, Trudy Cargill.
Except for Jesus, no one God-loved me more.

Contents

Along the Narrow Path

I grew up with a lot of rules. Most of the grievous ones to me came from the church: "Don't touch, don't look, don't go, don't have the wrong fun in the world." I do not think these rules were given to me with wrong motives. The purpose was to define and clarify what others thought God wanted from me in the way of my conduct. But many of the rules did not seem to be in the Bible. Does God want me to refrain from bowling? Or is reading a newspaper on Sunday profaning the Lord's Day? I have a real desire to please God with my conduct, to be a godly person. But that seems to be between me and the Lord and His commands. Jesus laid out a path that is difficult enough. This book came to mind because of insights I gained by studying two passages of Scripture.

> And one of them (Pharisees), an expert in the law, questioned Him (Jesus) to test Him, "Teacher, what commandment is greatest in the law?" And He said to him, "You shall love the Lord your God with your whole heart, and with your entire soul, and with all of your understanding. This is the great and first commandment. The second is similar; love your neighbor as yourself. On these two commandments hang the whole law and the prophets." —Matthew 22:35–40

> All things, therefore, that you wish men to do to you, do also to them; for this is the law and the prophets. Enter through the narrow gate. For wide is the gate and broad is the highway that leads to perdition, and

> there are many entering it. How narrow the gate and narrowed the road that leads to life! And few are those finding it. —Matthew 7:12–14

The "gate" and the "road" are obviously metaphors. The gate is Jesus Christ; we are saved by grace through faith in Him only. The road, or path, is how I walk every day with Jesus in integrity and accountability. If I let other people define the "gate" and the "road" with rules of conduct, I take up an onerous burden. When I let myself define the narrow way, self-justification takes over, and I miss the mark. When I learned from the teaching of Jesus and His apostles that every expectation of the Lord for my behavior is contained in loving God supremely and loving others sincerely, I found the "way," and it is glorious! My hope is that this devotional will help the reader find the "way" of true godliness and joy in following Jesus Christ.

Week 1

God-Love

Sunday: God-Love

Love is an English word that has many meanings and nuances that can only be understood from the context in which it is contained or by a modifying word that accompanies it. To say, "I love Jesus," is different from saying, "I love ice cream." Husbands and wives say they "make love," which carries an entirely different concept from when all Christians say, "We should love each other." *Love* is a word with many different meanings.

The original language of our New Testament is common Greek. It was everyone's second language in the days of Jesus and the Apostles. It is also the language of the Septuagint, the ancient Greek translation of the Old Testament, which is quoted in the New. Greek has several different words that we translate *love*. One describes the physical and ecstatic love of a man and a woman, another for the love for family, another for the love of people and things that please us. But the Scripture demands a word not found in other Greek literature: *agapé*. It is best understood in the context of John 3:16, "God loved the world so much that he gave His One and Only Son," and in 1 John 3:16, "By this we know love, that in our behalf Jesus laid down his life." Divine love; *God-love.* Having God-love is the only way we can walk the narrow path. So, in the devotions that follow, the Bible word *agapé* will be referred to both as "love" and "God-love."

> For this is the message that we have heard from the beginning, that we should God-love one another ... let us have God-love for one another, because love comes from God. —1 John 3:11; 4:7

God-love has emotion that goes with it. But it is primarily known by what we say and do. God-love is expressed as gratitude for the grace found in the sacrificial death of Jesus and is shown by obeying His commands and the teaching of His apostles. It is displayed toward others when we follow the command of Christ, "Do unto others as we would have done unto ourselves" (Matthew 7:12). It is shown to the world when we tell the good news about Jesus. God-love motivates us to imitate Jesus as He went around Galilee and Judea doing good because of His compassion for all people. It propels us down the narrow path.

> "Oh, Lord, thank You for loving me! I need to love like that! Pour out Your God-love on me so I can God-love in the same way. Forgive me, Lord, where I have not loved with God-love. In Jesus' name I pray. Amen."

Monday: The Straight and Narrow

If there is any story in the Bible that I identify with, it is the account of Jonah. I spent a good portion of my adult life running from God. There is not room in this devotion to give a full account of it. Jonah suffered three days in the belly of a fish until he came to repentance and obedience to God. I was there for twenty-five years. But God faithfully pursued me, and when I surrendered to His will and told Him I loved Jesus and He could do whatever He wanted with me, I was saved. It was not my doing but the grace of God. But there was still that fearful obstacle to faith that sent me running in the first place—the *straight and narrow*. To me, the straight and narrow represented a set of expectations for my behavior that was impossible to meet. But the constricted path is exactly the way in which Jesus wants me to walk and the narrow gate He has set as the beginning of my life in Him.

> All things, therefore, that you wish men to do to you, do also to them; for this is the law and the prophets. Enter through the narrow gate. For wide is the gate and broad is the highway that leads to perdition, and there are many entering it. How narrow the gate and narrow the road that leads to life! And few are those finding it. —Matthew 7:12–14

At first reading, many believers find this passage standing alone to be frightening because it may represent a challenge that we cannot meet, a measure of holiness that cannot be attained. But when we understand that the straight and narrow way is defined by God-love, we can leave behind the letter of the law or any old list of man-made rules. The narrow way becomes filled with light and possibility. *Love God supremely, and God-love others sincerely.*

"Thank You, Lord, for Your love to me. Fill me with God-love. Send the Holy Spirit to spread that love throughout my heart, soul, and mind. Infuse Your royal law into my being. Help me, Lord, to be obedient to the supreme command of Jesus: to love You supremely and God-love others sincerely. Amen."

Tuesday: Doctrines and Deeds

There are some plays and dramas I will never forget. One in particular is a comedy episode on a television program called *Mama's Family*. The episode was set in Mama's house where she and her daughter Eunice and son-in-law Ed entered after attending Sunday church. There seemed to be a glow on their faces as they came into the home in their Sunday-best clothing. The minister had preached on love, and they were repeating the words of the homily with the greatest of emotion and enthusiasm. "I *love* everyone! I have such *love* in my heart!" Since the preacher had told them that they should love their enemies, Eunice decided to call her sister and forgive her for all the rotten things her sister had done to her. Before that was over, Eunice was yelling at her sister and telling her that she and her kids were rotten. When Mama called her out for that, Ed came in to defend Eunice, and the fight was on. It was funny in a tragic way, but it illustrated that it is not enough to have the squishy emotion of love, or to believe in it, or go to a church where love is preached, or even write a book of devotions about it. It has to be more than that or it is not God-love. The Apostle John wrote, "Let us not God-love in our doctrine and what we say, but with deeds and in reality" (1 John 3:18).

God-love is an action word. If we say that we love Jesus, He said that we will obey His commands. If we have God-love toward others, we will always do what is right in our relationship and actions toward them with *sincerity*. I think I have to stop here and confess that I do not possess perfect God-love toward *everyone*. But the Holy Spirit helps me day by day to become more fruitful in God-love and His will. He helps us who are His children to stay on that straight and narrow path.

"Dear Lord, help me today to walk the straight and narrow way. Help me to show my God-love toward You by my obedience and by the way I treat my family and every person I interact with today. Forgive me, Lord, for my selfish actions and words. Fill me with Your Spirit at this moment that I may be perfect in God-love. Amen."

Wednesday: Me First

I know a young man who became one of those guys in the Coast Guard who jump out of helicopters into the freezing, storming water to rescue people who have no other hope. He is one of my contemporary heroes. Everyone should admire brave men and women who risk their own lives to save people in trouble. They do not care if we have done something really stupid to endanger our lives. They just come to the rescue, respecting our lives by endangering their own.

On the opposite end are the me-first people who have little respect for the lives of other humans. When this me-first attitude begins to rise within me I feel terribly condemned in my own spirit. Thank God for the Holy Spirit, who transforms my thinking and gives me courage to do what is right toward others.

What will happen when our culture loses all respect for the lives of people? Who will come to our rescue? Who will race toward gunfire to save the innocent? Who will run into a burning building if there is even a possibility to save a life? Who will love us in that way?

> But when we were weak, at just the right time Christ died for the ungodly. Maybe for a righteous person someone will die. For the benefit of a good person perhaps someone would even dare to die. But God declares His God-love to us what while we were still sinners, Christ died for us. —Romans 5:6–8

There is no better illustration of God-love than Jesus hanging on the Cross. This was His narrow path of obedience and the small gate the Father gave Him. There was no other way to save us out of this life and our predicament. Jesus placed our lives ahead of

His life, our benefit before His own. And to those who believe and receive Jesus, God has imparted His God-love in us so we can walk the narrow path reflecting that kind of love. There is no substitute in our spiritual life for God-love.

> "Lord, thank You for loving me enough to send Jesus to suffer and die for my benefit just to save me. My trouble is of my own making. I have made many foolish decisions, and the memory of my sins disturbs me. But You saved me, a sinner, because You love me. Such thoughts are wonderful to me. Help me to reflect God-love back to You and to others that I may walk the straight and narrow way. Amen."

Thursday: Perfection

No one is perfect except Jesus. I think that is what all reasonable people believe. No one is perfect in the sense of being flawless. But perfection is demanded of people every day. When I fly on commercial aircraft, I expect perfection from the pilots, especially on the landing. And everyone on the plane demands the crew be *perfectly sober*. The landing may be a little bumpy, but as long as we land safely without too much terror, it is "perfect."

I love to "fly" the flight simulator in my basement and have a lot of fun being a wannabe aviator. My desire for perfection in virtual aviation is often disappointed but never dangerous. Several of my friends are experienced commercial pilots and expect perfection of themselves because they feel great responsibility for their passengers. I greatly admire their ability to fly huge aircraft in a perfect manner. But I also know they are human and not flawless in all of their actions. So I tremble when I read in my Bible that Jesus orders me to be perfect.

> You are therefore to be perfect as your Father in heaven is perfect. —Matthew 5:48

This command of Jesus is so shocking to us that we tend to pass over the word *therefore* and fail to figure out what He is saying to us. But in verses 43–47 Jesus was teaching us to God-love our enemies and pray for them. God loved us before we ever loved Him. We treated Him as though He was our enemy, preferring to live in our sins instead of surrendering to His will and receiving a gift of grace. Jesus said God sends good things to both the just and the unjust. His offer of salvation is extended to all people who will have faith in Jesus. We may have to defend ourselves against our enemies, but we can pray for them and do unto them as we would have done unto us. We, as imperfect people, can have perfect actions when we apply God-love to everyone—whether they are friend or enemy, whether we like them or not. In God's eyes, this is perfection on the straight and narrow.

> "Father God, I need Your grace with this one. You know my worst enemy. I pray for this person that they will experience Your grace. I forgive them for whatever they may have done to harm me. Help me to be at peace with them. Shield me from harm. Show me how I may do something good for them and never return evil for evil. Help me to reflect Your God-love to them. In Jesus' name, amen."

Friday: Never-Ending Love

It is hard to think of eternity. Scientists used to think the material world was eternal, without beginning or end. This was the thinking of philosophers twenty-five hundred years ago. This idea persisted among scientists until the last half-century when advances in mathematics, astronomy, and theoretical physics demonstrated that the Bible is reliable in its assertions that the universe had a beginning and will have an end.

But we as ordinary folks knew this all along in a practical way. Nothing is forever in this world. Only in the next world can our existence continue with the reality of Jesus, or without. Everything we can see, hear, taste, smell, or touch is decaying and will inevitably pass away. Our bodies had their beginning in the womb, and since the age of twenty-five, we have been on a slow decline as our bodies waste away day by day, just as the Bible says. The same thing is true of human relationships. They are temporal and will not last beyond death. The Apostle Paul tells us of something that will last.

> God-love never fails. But if there be prophesies, they will be done away; whether tongues, they will cease; or knowledge, it will be destroyed. ... But now remains faith, hope, and God-love. The greatest of these is God-love. —1 Corinthians 13:8, 13

In heaven with Jesus and all of the redeemed, there will be no need of faith. We will have the object of our belief, so we will be able to see clearly all the mysteries of God. There will be no need to have hope, for all of our hopes will be fulfilled. But God-love will remain eternal, never-ending in relationship with God and the heavenly host. Jesus prayed for His disciples that they would receive God-love from the Father and so follow Jesus' command to God-love one another in this present age (John 17). And Paul testified, "The God-love of God has been lavishly poured out into our hearts by the Holy Spirit given to us" (Romans 5:5). It is the gift of God to those who have received His grace in Christ Jesus. So if we feel we are lacking anything in the way of God-love, we can ask Him who gives to His children without finding fault for asking.

> "Father, pour out Your God-love into my heart *lavishly* just as Paul says You do. I want never-ending love. Help me to live out God-love today with You and every person I come in contact with today. Amen."

Saturday: Quintessence

Philosophers have searched in their thinking for thousands of years for the "ground of being." Aristotle thought that there were four elements or foundations of the world that we understand by our five senses: air, earth, fire, and water. But what unified them in such perfect order? It is the fifth essence: the *quintessence.*

Astronomers, physicists, and biologists have supplanted philosophers in the search for the unifying theory for the ground of being, searching for it in the material world. With the advent of the great telescopes and the mathematics of Einstein we explore far into the universe virtually looking back in time to the beginnings of the universe.

But the more we delve toward the beginning with a materialistic perspective, the more questions arise about the origin of all things. Biologists have mapped the genome and can read and even manipulate the DNA book of life but cannot find where this information came from. Millions of words have been written about this. I am not a scientist or biologist, but I believe the quintessence has been found in three verses of Scripture.

> In Him (Jesus) we have redemption, the forgiveness of sins. He is the image of the unseen God, the firstborn of all creation. Because in Him was created everything in the heavens and on the earth, the visible and the invisible; whether thrones or angelic powers, whether rulers or authorities, all things have been created through Him and for Him. —Colossians 1:15–17

God-love is the quintessence of personal holiness, the essence of a godly life. Just as the love of God brought forth all creation, so too with God-love the Holy Spirit brings forth the holiness He commands. Jesus said all the laws of Moses and the teachings of the prophets and expectations for our godly behavior are summed up in this quintessence, "You shall love the Lord your God with all of your heart, soul, and mind, and your neighbor as yourself" (Matthew 22:37). If we lack this essence in any way, we can ask of God who gives to us liberally without finding fault for the asking.

> "Dear Lord, I need more of God-love. Fill me with the Holy Spirit today so that love will motivate my actions to obey the commands of Christ and do what is right to others. Purify me that I may receive this blessing. In Jesus' name I pray, amen."

Week 2:

Difficulties

Sunday: The Difficult Way

Nothing worth doing is ever easy. I have held this to be a law ever since my eighteenth birthday when Father left me at college one spring day with five bucks in my pocket, a summer job I started the next day, and a room at my Grandma's house I shared with my cousin. Dad said, "Good luck, Son" and then asked for my set of keys to the family car. I was not angry or disappointed because I knew he did the best he could. My siblings told me later he pulled the car over to the side of the road and cried like a baby. But as I watched the taillights of Dad's Pontiac disappear along with my family, I realized that everything from now on would be up to me—even eating.

The following months at college taught me that I was not unique, and there were many other people in the same type of situation. Some of my friends made it through, and some did not. Since that time the best solutions to the problems of my life have been the more difficult options, the better jobs the more problematic, the best bosses the most demanding, the narrow trail the most rewarding. Jesus said:

> Enter through the narrow gate. For wide is the gate and broad is the highway that leads to perdition, and there are many entering it. How narrow the gate and narrowed the road that leads to life! And few are those finding it." —Matthew 7:13–14

These words of Jesus came from His Sermon on the Mount. The words are not easier to receive today than they were back then, but each of us needs to take them to heart. This command is from a sermon of Jesus in Matthew chapters 5–7, describing how one follows Jesus with God-love. Do we negate the great saving principles of grace and faith by saying the commands of

18

Jesus are *not optional*? Never. Jesus gave His commands that we may live an abundant and holy life, which is pleasing to Him. He also said that every expectation that heaven has for our integrity is contained in two great commandments, "You shall love God supremely and love others sincerely" (see Matthew 22:36–39). God-love. To love that way puts us on a narrow path, sometimes filled with trouble and difficulty, to a large reward.

> "Father in heaven, help me to be obedient to the command of Christ. Teach me the narrow path; put me in the difficult way; show me the small gate. May Your Spirit be strong in me when I am weak. Amen."

Monday: The Pickle Trail

It was called the Pickle Trail for a reason. It happened to be the shortest trail and the most difficult in the state park where I went with the church for an outing. I had almost reached my sixty-ninth birthday. The sign at the beginning of the trail warned of the difficulty of the trail and particularly warned off senior citizens and small children. Exercise by walking and riding a bicycle gave me some confidence in my ability to hike the trail. But age takes a toll on our strength and endurance no matter how we strive to stay strong. Part of the trail ran along a rocky creek and the smooth round stones that covered the trail were slippery and hard on my feet. At several points I had to climb over boulders. The young people scampered right up. They offered to help me, but I was determined to navigate the whole trail. I had to go up over the boulders on my hands and knees and scoot down on my butt. When the trail left the creek, it became smoother but went up the side of the mountain in a series of switchbacks. I began praying not to die as I climbed to the top. The young people did not abandon me but, bored with my slow progress, ran up and down the trail laughing and having a great time. I was barely walking when I finished. Everything hurt. But the joy of the difficult way filled my heart.

> We are fixing our eyes on Jesus, the originator and finisher of our faith, who for the joy set before Him endured the cross. —Hebrews 12:2

God chose the difficult way for Jesus. He has also marked out a narrow, difficult way for us. Jesus said we should love God supremely and God-love others sincerely and act out our lives according to those principles. This is where the difficulty comes in. Extending grace and forgiveness to others is difficult; loving our enemies is even harder. Obeying Jesus is many times not what we want. God-love sometimes takes all we have. But therein is great joy.

> "Lord, I need Your Spirit to accomplish the deeds of God-love. Help me to be obedient. Help me to God-love others as I love myself. Remind me how Jesus loves me and found joy in the difficult way so that I could be saved. Praise the name of Jesus! Amen."

Tuesday: Isolation

Trying to walk the narrow path of God-love sometimes makes me feel isolated. It seems as though no one in this world wants to walk that narrow path. There is so much that is anti-God-love among the affairs of this world that it sometimes seems as though I am all alone.

This feeling of isolation can be discouraging when we are going against the current of culture. When I feel judgmental about that, the Lord reminds me of my less-than-loving words and actions and my own need of grace. But there is a huge dissonance between people who are trying to follow Jesus Christ on the straight and narrow and a materialistic culture that pursues happiness by chasing money and pleasure. It seems impossible to be in tune with the people with whom I engage every day. The media constantly bombards me with violence, sensuality, and secularism, portraying people like me as stupid and evil. But I have to be involved in the culture for the sake of those who need to hear about the gospel. Without neglecting my mission to bring the word of salvation to the world, I really need to spend some time with people whose thinking, desires, and aspirations are in harmony with mine. I need to love and be loved. This has always been a problem for Christians. The Apostle Peter wrote to the early church about this.

> Beloved, I call upon you as sojourners and exiles to abstain from lusts of the flesh with war against the soul, having good conduct among the Gentiles. When they speak against you as evildoers, they will observe your good works and glorify God in the day of visitation. —1 Peter 2:11–12

Jesus did not establish a go-it-alone religion. He founded the church, a community of believers. There may be a few who found a way to practice and receive God-love by living alone in a cave or sitting for years on the top of a pillar without coming down. (This was actually done by a fifth-century monk named Simeon Stylites.) But most followers of Jesus Christ have found that being a part of a community of believers is much better for us than isolation. We all need to practice God-love in our culture and in a community of faith in order to receive God-love that comes to us from the company of other Christians.

> "Father, I thank You for my friends in Christ. I love my brothers and sisters in the church. Thank You, Lord, for the God-love I receive from them. I thank You, for You have transformed their lives and infused God-love into them for their benefit and mine. Amen."

Wednesday: Hostility

One time I was making a hospital call on a member of my congregation. As I was walking down the hall and passing by other rooms, I heard someone call out, "George!" It was someone I had known years before when I was not trying to walk the straight and narrow. When I told him that Jesus had saved me and made me a pastor, his mouth fell open, and he said, "George, I did not think such a thing was possible."

I thought everyone would be pleased, even *very* pleased, when I came to true repentance and began following Jesus. Not so. I was not surprised that people were skeptical of my profession of faith considering my prior conduct and the way I had hurt people. Not that I was a violent man, but I was very selfish and said whatever came to my mind whether it hurt people or not. I was in the grip of the old sinful nature and freely lived that out doing whatever my body told me to do.

I knew I would have to prove myself in displaying the change that grace brought to me. I thought *everyone* would be for *that*. To my surprise I found opposition, even hostility, to my efforts to live out a life of God-love. Coworkers constantly watched me and pointed out every inconsistency, no matter how small or imagined. I thank God for my family who, after a time of watching me, has fully supported me. I have found others who walk with me on the straight and narrow. This seems to be the key to surviving a culture that will ever oppose us. When we have companions on the narrow path, the hostility of the world has little effect.

> Two are better than one ... For if either of them falls, the one will lift up his companion. But woe to the one who falls when there is not another to lift him up. — Ecclesiastes 4:9-10 NASB

Even with the Holy Spirit as our helper, believers really do need each other. Research has shown that Christians who are a regular part of a small support group, such as a Bible study, are the most successful of believers. Even the largest congregations have small groups. Ask God to direct you to a good one, and you will be blessed and shielded from the hostility of this world.

> "Lord, direct my steps down the narrow path to some other of Your servants that we may walk together. May I God-love them. Give me grace that I may receive love from them. Amen."

Thursday: Temptation

Temptation never bothered me while I was doing everything my body wanted me to do. When I took God's name in vain and worse, the devil never interrupted me. He seemed to be pleased with my addictions and excesses. As long as the flesh ran rampant, there was peace with the evil one. But when the new birth arrived and the grace of God transformed my life, the devil went to work. Whatever is in the heart of the devil, it is the antithesis to God-love. He hates God and His children with Him. Whatever God has done, the devil wants to destroy. Suddenly, temptation became a problem to me, and I began to understand that it is a form of persecution that produces great suffering. Everyone in Christ undergoes temptation just as Jesus Himself was tempted and tested by the devil. We are constantly tempted to abandon the narrow path.

> Be sober, watch carefully. Your enemy, the devil, walks around like a roaring lion, seeking those whom he may devour. Stand against him, strong in faith, knowing that the same sufferings are being laid upon your brethren who are in the world. Now the God of all grace who called you into His eternal glory in Christ, after you have suffered for a little while, will Himself restore, confirm, strengthen, and establish you. —1 Peter 5:8–10

It is a fight for all of us. Even Jesus suffered temptation in every way just as we all do (Hebrews 2:18). Yet, He was victorious against every wile of the devil. When we have been blessed with grace and the presence of the Holy Spirit, we have strength that does not reside in those who are clueless about God. There is victory for us if we hold fast to faith and God-love for Him and others. Besides, like the apostle tells us, the most intense of temptations are gone after a little while. It is the promise from God that we will have the comfort, strength, and steadfastness of Christ to help us.

> "Oh Father, strengthen the God-love in me when I am tempted to sin against You and others. Help me to endure the intense testing that comes my way. You said in Your Word, 'God-love never fails' (1 Corinthians 13:8). I need Your love, God. Restore, strengthen, and establish me that I may live with God-love toward You and others. Amen."

Friday: Failures

Failures in life have often served me very well. Not that I *want* to fail or mess up my life or harm anyone. Some of the failures caused huge damage to myself and others, even those I claimed to love. I thank God and His grace that I did not have the failures that ruin, the ones that end life and freedom.

But those failures that come when we are trying to accomplish something, learn something new, or try to walk the narrow way with God-love, tell us the present limits of our ability, understanding, and love. With prayer and faith in God, the steps to success seem to be *try and fail; try again, fail again; try again, fail again; try again, succeed; try again, improve; try continually to improve, become proficient.*

The grace of God and the help of the Holy Spirit gives me great resolve to love God supremely and others sincerely despite my failures. So, when I fall short of the standard of God-love, I call upon the Lord and try again.

> Now may our Father God and our Lord Jesus direct our way to you. And may the Lord cause you to increase abundantly and overflow with God-love to one another and everyone, exactly as we do to you ... for you are taught by God to God-love one another, as indeed you do for the brothers in all Macedonia. But we call upon you to excel even more. —1 Thessalonians 3:11–12; 4:9–10

Paul wrote to the church at Thessalonica to praise them for their successes in faith, good works, and God-love. But they had failures also. It seems to be a never-ending effort for us to succeed in God-love. Winston Churchill once gave a message that repeated three words, "Never give in." We must never give in to failure, never let sin stand between us and God. Every time we stumble on the path of God-love we must call out to the source of grace and God-love. If we feel that we are walking steadfastly on the path, we should pray to Him that we may excel even more.

> "God, You are continually teaching me to walk the path of God-love. Even my failures are not failures to You but rather an opportunity to teach me and help me to recover, improve, and excel in God-love. Fill me with the Holy Spirit, and teach me new ways that I may love today. Amen."

Saturday: Slavery

Every one of us who is trying to walk the narrow path with God-love understands the struggle between good and evil that resides in each one of us. I have found that it is *impossible* to walk the narrow path of God-love if I am a slave to sin. Jesus Christ must set me free. From the womb, we are rebels against God. No God-love there. This is the reason we seem to be powerless against the desires, temptations, and the anti-God-love actions that plague us.

Describing what it was like to be bound up by sin, Paul asked a rhetorical question and supplied an answer. "What a miserable man I am! Who will free me from the body of this death? I thank God through Jesus Christ my Lord" (Romans 7:24–25). I know what it is like to be a slave, to be bound up by the sin principle and pushed around by it, defeated at every turn. I still have temptations, faults, and sometimes failure. But I have been a slave to sin, and I have been freed. I know the difference that Jesus Christ can make. It is infinitely better to be free to love as God intended. My confidence in writing this is the knowledge that if I can be set free, anyone can be liberated! Paul tells us how.

> What then? May we sin because we are not under law but under grace? May that never happen! Do you not know that you are the slaves of whomever you present yourselves for obedience? Whether of sin resulting in death or obedience unto righteousness? ... For just as you presented your bodies as slaves to impurity and to lawlessness on top of lawlessness, so now present your bodies as slaves to righteousness resulting in holiness. —Romans 6:15–16; 19

When we do what the inspired apostle has written to us in God-love, we understand that we can humble ourselves before the Almighty, emptying ourselves of self-will and pride, to be set free to love as Jesus Christ has commanded us. What glory and peace will go with us on the straight and narrow!

> "Lord, here I am today! I give my body, mind, and soul to You at this moment so that I may be free to love You supremely and others sincerely. Jesus, You said that, 'If the Son sets you free, you are free indeed' (John 8:36). I claim that promise at this moment. Fill me with the Spirit that the chains of sin may be broken so that I may be free to possess the God-love that is overflowing and abundant. Amen."

Week 3

Happy on the Narrow Path

Sunday: Have a Good Day

How many times have I told someone, or been told, to have a good day? I think everyone wants to have a good day, even the people who seldom have one. We want to be happy. But there are bad days too, and I seem to remember them more than the good. Some days are good, happy days, but some are not.

Sometimes people will tell me, "Have a blessed day," which means, "I am a Christian, and I hope that you have a happy day in the Lord." I am truly blessed when I have a blessed-happy day in the Lord. I feel one with Him; my spirit is at peace, and it seems easy to walk the straight and narrow with God-love. But there are days when I really don't feel spiritual or even Christian. Where is the love? Where is the happiness?

Jesus talked about how to live spiritually happy. The original word used to describe blessed happiness in the Sermon on the Mount is most often just translated "blessed." A good way to think of it is "blessed-happy." Blessed! Jesus began His sermon with what are called the Beatitudes, and ended it with an illustration.

> Blessed-happy are the poor in spirit ... those who mourn ... the gentle ... those who hunger and thirst for righteousness ... the merciful ... the pure in heart ... the peacemakers ... the persecuted ... Therefore everyone who hears these words of Mine and practices them will be just like a wise man who built his house upon a rock." —Matthew 5:3–10; 7:24

By actually putting the principles of God-love into daily practice in our lives, we can live "blessed-happy" along the straight and narrow. We can be blessed even when the circumstances of life say we are cursed. Although we are mourning, or have been hurt, or are undergoing persecution, or just when we don't feel blessed, our faith in God will not be destroyed or our confidence in His grace diminished because of our love for God. Blessed-happiness brings the peace that escapes the understanding of those who do not know Jesus like we who follow Him in God-love along the narrow path.

> "Dear Lord, I want to live a happy-blessed life. Your love carries me along every day. Help me to put the principles of Jesus to work in my life that I may gain His wisdom and share in His happiness. Forgive me where I have fallen short. I want my life to be founded on the Rock of My Salvation, Jesus. Amen."

Monday: Poor in Spirit

No one I know of wants to be poor. We may not want to be rich, but we certainly do not want to be poor. We like to eat, have warm shelter, and be clothed. When I think about it, I do not want to be poor in spirit *either*. I want to be spirited and confident, able to handle situations that come my way. If any bad, difficult, or stressful thing comes my way, I want to be able to deal with it.

My preference in a church is one that has spirited worship with loud singing and praises to God. I find it difficult to be around people who are dour and pessimistic. As a shepherd I try to encourage and enrich those sheep who have a poverty of joy. Except for a medical problem of depression, I can see no reason for living life always depressed and doubtful. We who have received grace have the hope of eternal life! But Jesus said something that I must believe, understand, and practice if I want to walk the straight and narrow with God-love.

> Spiritual-happy are the poor in spirit, for theirs is the kingdom of the heavens. —Matthew 5:3

The poverty Jesus spoke about does not have anything to do with money, success, material possessions, or the lack of them. It is about poverty of *spirit.* But He does not speak of self-loathing or a deficiency of confidence. Jesus speaks of those who are not proud before God. Pride is the original sin of humankind. Adam and Eve were presented with a choice that confronted them with God's way or their way. Instead of God's command, they listened to the tempter who said, "You can be your own god and decide for yourself what is good and evil. Your way is better than God's way. If you will eat the forbidden fruit, you will be the only god you will ever need." He tempted them to love themselves more than they loved God. Pride.

When we are poor in spirit, we humble ourselves before God and say, "You are God, and I am not. I am nothing without You. I cannot save myself." Jesus said when we are poor in spirit all the spiritual blessings of the heavens are ours to claim. We can be blessed-happy and confident in the love of God when we are poor in spirit.

> "Lord God, thank You for the grace and love You have given me. You are my God, and I will bow to Your will. I am nothing without You. Bless me, Lord, with heavenly blessings today. Amen."

Love the Narrow Path

Tuesday: Under Control

One of the great stories about Alexander the Great is how he acquired his great war horse, Bucephalus. The name means "ox-head," which referred to the misshapen head of the mighty stallion. When Prince Alexander was a young teen, his father King Philip paid a fortune for the steed. But no matter what they did, the king's trainers could not tame Bucephalus or break him to receive a rider. One day Alexander watched while the men tried throughout the day to break the wildness of the beast to no avail. "I can tame him," he boldly told his frustrated father. King Philip laughed, "Boy, if you can tame him, you can have him."

But young Alexander had noticed something about Bucephalus; he was spooked by his own shadow. So Alexander pointed the horse at the setting sun, jumped on his back and rode his new mount out of sight. Bucephalus became one of the most famous horses of all time. Alexander was one to be in the front of the battle, and Bucephalus proved to be a brave and mighty warrior. There were no saddles in those days, so Alexander fought bareback. In the midst of the chaos and noise of battle, Bucephalus responded to the slightest pressure of Alexander's knees, a word spoken, a tug on the mane, or a kick of the heels.

The Greeks had a word to describe the disposition of a mighty animal who is brought under the control of his master: *praus*. This word means to have a temperament of gentleness and meekness that accepts the directions of the master without resisting. The Bible uses the word in the third Beatitude.

> Blessed-happy are the gentle [*praus*], for they shall inherit the earth. —Matthew 5:5

38

We cannot walk the straight and narrow of God-love if the "wildness" of our heart is unbroken. What a blessing it is when we are brought under the control of the Master. Our strengths are liberated from our fears, passions, and strong desires to walk the narrow way with God-love. The power of our body, mind, and soul are reigned in and taken under control. What happiness comes to us when our wild heart is tamed by God.

> "Dear Lord, thank You for breaking me to Your control. Your training makes me happy! I surrender to You. Take away my fears. Bring gentleness into my life. Will You make me strong and powerful in Your kingdom of God-love? In Jesus' name, amen."

Wednesday: Grief

No one who has gained much age in this world has escaped seasons of mourning. Death is an unavoidable part of the human predicament, and grief follows for the living. Some of the best and most difficult experiences in ministry come around funerals. Grief tests our God-love. At such times, I have seen families bound together tightly by the God-love they have for one another, and I have seen other families torn apart by anger at God, selfishness, and recrimination. Some people gain faith, but in some, faith is lost.

When Jesus said, "Blessed-happy are the ones mourning, for they shall be comforted" (Matthew 5:4), it is difficult at first to understand how it is possible to be blessed in grief or how we will be comforted. When I have officiated at funerals, the Lord has been faithful to prompt me to preach the gospel of Jesus Christ at some point in the sermon. It is a moment when the whole congregation is contemplating their own mortality. With love, it is the perfect time to tell people about the hope we have in Jesus Christ so that they may be blessed with comforting wisdom.

> It is better to go to a house of mourning than to go to a house of feasting, because that is the end of every man, and the living takes it to heart. —Ecclesiastes 7:2 NASB

Why is it better for us to go to a funeral than to a party? Wisdom. At a party we try to forget the worries of life. At a funeral we are acutely aware of the frailty of life, and we come to an understanding of the fact that we are mortal. It is essential that we go through a time of grieving when we lose someone we love. But we who follow Jesus in God-love down the narrow path find *comfort* in the *wisdom* that God gives. We know God loves us, and there is hope that will carry us through this life into the next. This wisdom comforts us when we mourn the death of a loved one, because we can entrust them to a loving God who is perfectly just and perfect in mercy.

> "Father in Heaven, thank You for the life that you have given me. Thank You for the life that has been given to those I love. Help me, Lord, when I grieve; comfort me when I lose them. And help me so live that when I die, those who have loved me will praise You, the God of all mercy, for Your grace in my life. Amen."

Thursday: What We Want

A couple of years ago I was able to go to a major PGA golf tournament. The middle of August did not seem to be a good time to have a tournament in the Midwest. The heat and humidity were stifling. The directors allowed each person to bring in only one water bottle from outside the tournament, as they wanted to sell me everything I wanted in the way of refreshments while at the tournament. My bottle lasted no time.

After observing the play for a while, I realized I was *really* thirsty. I went to one of the several food pavilions and turned away when I saw the very long line snaking far out onto the path. *No worries*, I thought, *I will go to another one.* Same result. The places that had a fountain to fill my water bottle had similar queues. I finally decided to stop walking and just wait in one of the lines. It seemed none of them were in the shade, and there was nowhere to sit down. Being a septuagenarian, I was not only thirsty, I was in trouble.

Thank God I got some water before I collapsed! The great turnaround in my life happened when I began thirsting for the love of God and the righteousness of Jesus Christ and stopped thirsting after the desires of my body and the things of this world. I found blessed-happiness.

> Blessed-happy are those who hunger and thirst for righteousness, for they shall be fully satisfied. — Matthew 5:6

We generally get what we really want or get busted in the process. Whether it is the appetites of flesh, money, or love, we will do everything in our power to get what we really want. We live frustrated because much of what we strive for in this life cannot be fulfilled in the way we want. The greatest disillusionments in life come when we do get what we want, and it does not satisfy. A greater emptiness comes to us than before we had the object of our desire. Jesus teaches us that to desire righteousness with all of our being will bring full satisfaction. Righteousness means being in right God-loving relationship with Jesus Christ. God provides that by His grace and love for us *when we really want it.*

> "Father, I pray the prayer of the Psalmist, 'As the deer pants for the water brooks, so my soul pants for You, O God' (Psalm 42:1 NASB). I pray right now that I may be filled with the righteousness of Christ and God-love for You and others. Fill me now, Lord, by Your grace. Amen."

Friday: No Mercy

I believe that God-love is not only the solution to our personal relationship problems but also the answer to the relationship problems of our communities, nations, and governments. Missouri is my adopted home, and I have lived in this state for many years and love the people. I have become interested in the history of this state, particularly during the Civil War. It was a border state where many battles were fought, and the population was divided. No one was neutral. It was often neighbor against neighbor, even sometimes brother against brother. During the war and for several years after, the innocent people of the state were harassed and victimized by federal and confederate forces, pro-secession resistance fighters known as "bushwhackers," and numerous militia groups operating with approval of the government. From what I have found in my research, no one showed mercy to their opponents. From the Ozarks to the border with Arkansas, Missouri became a dangerous, poverty-stricken, and unhappy land. No mercy. Jesus said something about this.

"Blessed-happy are the merciful, for they shall receive mercy" (Matthew 5:7).

Jesus spoke to the strong and powerful, not to the weak and powerless. Mercy is forbearance toward someone over whom we have power or judgment. It is how we have been treated by a just God whose judgment is perfectly tempered by mercy. It is by the mercy and grace of a loving God that we find ourselves on the narrow path. He has filled our lives with blessedness, peace, and happiness we do not deserve. His Spirit encourages us when we walk through the difficult parts and rejoices with us in our blessings. He is a blessing to us.

Jesus said that mercy is measured back to the merciful. I hope Missouri never returns to those awful days of no mercy. I hope our families, brothers and sisters in the Lord, communities, nation, and the whole world will be blessed by the mercy we extend.

"Lord God, make me a blessing. I thank You for the mercy and grace that came into my life. You paid a supreme price for my well-being. Increase God-love in me so that I will show mercy to others. May your mercy and kindness be found in me that I can be a blessing of mercy to someone today. Make the happiness of others of supreme importance to me so in some measure I may reflect Your glory. Amen."

Saturday: Purity on the Way

Impure actions in my life always began with an impure thought that presents me with a choice. Temptation brings me to a point of decision leading to action that is either sinful or righteous. This cascade of thought-to-action is often triggered by what I see, hear, or feel. It is the way I am made. In the end, I cannot claim, "The devil made me do it," but I must admit that I do what I do because I choose to do it. To say otherwise is self-destructive denial. The Bible uses the heart as a metaphor of the will. My heart is the key to all of my actions, and the gauge of purity. Jesus taught that the issues of life come from the motives and intentions of the heart.

> Blessed-happy are the pure in heart, for they shall perceive God. —Matthew 5:8

> For the good man from the good wealth of his heart produces good things, and the evil man from an evil heart produces bad things; for from the overflow of the heart the mouth speaks. —Luke 6:45

Jesus taught us that every action toward God and others begins in our mind and is regulated by our heart. When our heart is corrupted by sin, we find that right conduct and the desires of the flesh are at war, and we seem unable to act with God-love in obedience to Him or in God-love toward others. We then are awash with guilt, and we do not feel happy or blessed either one. But God gives His Holy Spirit to us so that our hearts may be purified (Acts 15:8–9), dispersing God-love throughout our hearts (Romans 5:5).

With a pure heart our will is free to act out with God-love toward Him and other human beings. What happiness to have a clear conscience day by day in deed and word! If we humble ourselves before God and ask Him, He will give the Holy Spirit that we may have a pure heart and our actions can be motivated by God-love. We will walk on the straight and narrow way.

> "Dear Father in Heaven, I want a pure heart. I cannot cleanse my own heart. Will You do Your work in me? Increase and overflow my heart with Your love! I believe Your Word in the Bible. I have faith in Your promise to give me the Holy Spirit. My faith is in You. Amen."

Week 4

Monsters on the Way

Sunday: Forktongue the Pleasant

Forktongue seems to be a harmless fellow that simply wants to engage us with innocent helpful advice. He can appear to us as Satan himself, whispering in our ear, or come to us as one of his servants. Forktongue never shows up when I am succeeding in God-love, when joy is in my heart because of the near presence of God. Satan truly is like a snake coiled in the path waiting to bite those who stumble upon him unaware of his presence. But Forktongue never presents as a snake. Rather, he seems a reasonable counselor with his deadly fangs, hidden until the right moment. This is the monster that conversed with our Lord in the days of His temptation, when the Spirit drove Jesus into the wilderness. We do not know how long Forktongue waited to strike. But it was not until Jesus became very hungry, thirsty, and weak. The twin fangs of Forktongue are the two-letter word *if.*

> And the tempter came beside and said to Him (Jesus), "*If* You are the Son of God, speak to these stones that they may become bread. ... *If* You are the Son of God, throw Yourself down (from the pinnacle of the Temple), and He will command His angels and upon their hands they will catch You. ... *If* You will fall down and worship me, I will give You everything." — Matthew 4:3–9

The implication of Forktongue to Jesus was, "If You really are the Son of God, why are You hungry? If You are the Son of God, why did He throw You out into this horrid place to starve to death? If You are the Son of God, why don't You have it all?" Similarly, Forktongue comes near to us and says, "If you really are the child of God, why are you sick? Why are finances so bad? Why did your beloved die? Why did you sin and fail God?" Forktongue comes to us in times of weakness and tries to *destroy our confidence* in the love of God and His grace by trying to talk us off the narrow way with his weasel-talk. Jesus came back at him with Scripture and, prayerfully, we should do the same.

> "Father, who will separate me from Your Love? Will crushing pressure from this world, or distress of mind, or persecution, hunger, nakedness, or danger destroy my confidence in Your love? No! Because I am more than a conqueror through Jesus Christ who loves me and gave Himself for me (Romans 8:35–39). My confidence in Your grace remains unshaken. Thank You, Lord. Amen."

Monday: Memine the Selfish

Every human being takes their first steps in life following Memine on the *anti-love* path. No one begins on the narrow path of God-love. Born in a broken world, our natural inclinations are rebellion and selfishness, the very characteristics of Memine the Selfish. We find familial love when we are nurtured, romantic love when our bodies mature, and we learn to *like-love* those people who please us.

If we have received Jesus in faith, we have received the love of God. But anti-God-love is the original sin of humanity and Memine the Selfish poisons to one degree or another the love for God and others that may be in our soul. Selfishness and rebellion against God eventually spawn greed, lust, hatred, murder, and war. The anti-love must be broken in us before we can walk the narrow path of God-love with integrity. Memine must die. Our self-will love, our anti-love, must be offered to God and crucified as an offering to Him. When we do that, the Holy Spirit of God increases our God-love for others to establish us on the narrow path. This is how the Apostle Paul prayed for the Christians of Thessalonica.

> May God our Father and our Lord Jesus direct our way to you. May the Lord multiply abundantly your God-love for one another and for everyone even as we have God-love for you, so that you may be established in your hearts blameless in the presence of our Lord Jesus with all His holy saints. Amen. —1 Thessalonians 3:11–13

It is easy to understand that we live in an evil anti-God-love world. Just reading a newspaper or watching some of the news will confirm this fact over and over. The harder thing for me to do is recognize the anti-love that dwells in my own being. All I can do is offer my self-will to God for cleansing and receive a gift of God-love. This is the first step down the narrow path.

> "Father in Heaven, as Your apostle prayed, I pray. I pray I would increase and overflow with God-love so that I may be presented blameless in the presence of Jesus and all His holy ones. Establish my heart, oh God, in Your love. May God-love rule and guide me. Will You teach me the ways of God-love? Will You make it real in my life? Take my anti-love away, Lord, so that God-love may be supreme. In the name of Jesus, I pray. Amen."

Tuesday: The Mad Inquisitor

I don't think there is anything that can destroy a church as quickly as a judgmental attitude among the people of the congregation. The Mad Inquisitor takes me off of the narrow path of God-love and, in Jesus' eyes, makes me a condemning hypocrite. Everyone recognizes, and hates, that "holier than thou," condemning attitude of this monster. It is easy to become judgmental about it. I know I can condemn the bad things in people that I refuse to see in myself.

It is the attitude that judges every observable flaw in others and refuses to give anyone any slack. God wants me to boldly stand up for truth. I must proclaim what sin is and how destructive it is to people. I know what sin is, whether I see it in myself or others. But my job is not to condemn others. My job is to tell them of the mercies and forgiveness that are in Jesus Christ and to be merciful and forgiving myself. I must speak of the grace of God and speak about a good and godly way of life, walking the path of God-love, free of the sins and the strong lusts of this world.

> Do not condemn so that you will not be condemned. For with what judgment you judge, you will be judged, and the yardstick you use to measure others will be used to measure you also. And why do you see the speck that is in the eye of your brother and do not think about the beam that is in your own eye? Or how can you say to your brother, "Let me take the speck out of your eye," and look, there is a beam in your eye? Hypocrite, first take the beam out of your eye, and then you will be able to see clearly to take the speck out of the eye of your brother. —Luke 6:42

A merciful attitude rather than a judgmental attitude, merciful words rather than condemnation, a forbearing spirit rather than unforgiveness, is what Jesus wants to see in us. When we see sin in ourselves or others, it should be addressed with a redemptive effort, not a condemning one. It makes us in a small measure like God, walking the narrow path with God-love.

> "Father in heaven, do not let me forget that You lifted me out of the mire of sin, that there was grace and mercy for me. So, instead of condemning and judging, let me give people a word of hope in Jesus Christ. Pour out Your Spirit upon me today, that I may reflect Your mercy and grace. Thank You, oh Lord! In Jesus' name, amen."

Wednesday: Apollyon the Destroyer

One of the most frustrating things to me is when we send our youth off to some secular university where their faith will be tested in many ways. Before long they will attract the attention of Apollyon the Destroyer or one of his acolytes (see Revelation 9:11). Some professor will think it is their calling to identify the Christian students in order to call them out and destroy their faith. Such warriors for Apollyon usually have more degrees than Fahrenheit and believe they can do the thinking for the rest of us.

Through such professors, Apollyon presents himself as being very wise and the only source of truth and reality that will brook no pushback from students. The basis of *everything* that this monster imposes on his victims is the assumption that there is no God. If God does not exist, there is no basis for morality, no basis for God-love, no basis for our existence except an *impossible* accident. Being wise in his own eyes, Apollyon's worldview of philosophy, ethics, science, politics, entertainment, and love is spouted with a constant atheistic screed throughout academia. He has drawn many victims away from the narrow path. The destroyer wants us all to ignore the fact that in these days, true science and the Bible converge more and more on the side of God. I thank God for being God and the Bible that informs me of His power and glory!

> They who dwell in the ends of the earth stand in awe of Your signs; You make the dawn and the sunset shout for joy. You visit the earth and cause it to overflow; You greatly enrich it; the stream of God is full of water; You prepare their grain, for thus You prepare the earth. —Psalm 65:8–9 NASB

This is the thing that we who have received God-love know. We have been transformed in our minds and hearts so that we can love Him back. We know that He is the *One who is*. When we have been touched by the infinite, it does not matter what kind of propaganda is pushed on us or what deception is thrown our way in the name of science or reason, that is neither scientific nor reasonable. Jesus prayed that the Father would protect us from the evil one so that we would remain in His love. Nothing can detach us from His God-love when we God-love Him.

> "God, what I believe does not stand on the words of humans. By Your Word and Your God-love I have faith. You have said that the just shall live by their faith. Help me, Lord, to faithfully walk the narrow way with pure God-love. Thank You, Lord, for Your Word, the source of truth. Amen."

Thursday: Fangar the Terrible

Only God-love can defeat this monster that stalks the path. Some of the worst decisions I have made in life have been because of this giant. He attacks with a combination of fear and anger. I see this dangerous beast at work in politics, religion, and violent acts of people from verbal assault to warfare. I seem to be particularly vulnerable to attack when I see injustice and other evils in this world. Fangar seems to be able to manipulate me into unloving acts and words when he injects fear into the situations that make me angry. He often starts with anxiety, building fear, then stoking anger and roiling up rage. When I confessed to a friend that I struggled this way with anger, he pointed me to Psalm 37. I am often in this passage of Scripture giving my angst up to the Lord, who helps me love those who are unlovely.

> Rest in the LORD and wait patiently for Him; do not fret because of him who prospers in his way, because of the man who carries out wicked schemes. Cease from anger and forsake wrath; do not fret; it leads only to evildoing. For evildoers will be cut off, but those who wait for the LORD, they will inherit the land. —Psalm 37:7–9 NASB

Fear combined with anger is the way agitators and manipulators move people to drastic action. Fangar has corrupted the noblest intentions of Christians. Think of the crusades, where the actions that began as a defense against hegemony and to protect Christians traveling to Jerusalem ended up with the commission of unspeakable atrocities as bad as those of the enemy. Fear and anger are a lethal combination. The Bible has all kinds of warnings about returning evil for evil. But God is faithful to help us to rest in Him and wait patiently for His justice. Then we will be able to resist evil and injustice with God-love and keep our integrity. He will make the rightness of our cause shine like the sun.

> "Thank You, Lord, for Your faithfulness. Help me to seek justice and truth without anger and fear. Help me, Lord, to never return evil for evil, but as much as possible return good for evil. Lord, assist me to protect the innocent, to do what is just and to act without rage. In Jesus' name, amen."

Friday: Theristēs the Dark Reaper

There is nothing that will challenge our God-love like the tragic or untimely death of a loved one or friend. Theristēs, which is the Greek word for *reaper*, is no respecter of race, religion, age, wealth, or beauty. He strikes quickly, or slowly over a time of sickness.

The most difficult of situations that a pastor encounters are the untimely deaths of people. At those times it is impossible for loved ones left behind not to ask, "Does God even care?" There are no medicines or any platitudes that will help, so I have found it best just to sit with mourners, cry with them, and pray that God would help me to help them some way.

The only reason I can figure out anything out about why we have to die is that we are born. One for one: one life, one death. It is the human predicament that I have an unavoidable appointment with Theristēs. Sadly, some abandon the narrow way because of the work of this monster. But my heart swells with God-love when I think that Jesus was *born*. That meant He was subjected to death, and a seemingly untimely one as well, although we know He died at just the right time. God shares the pain and sorrow of humanity because He participated with us in death. And He sent Jesus so that we could have hope in the midst of tragedy and death.

> For as in Adam all die, so also in Christ all will be made alive. —1 Corinthians 15:22 NASB

It is with hope that we survive Theristēs the Dark Reaper. In human terms it may seem as though this monster wins every time. But in Christ He is defeated every time. Our hope in the resurrection keeps us loving God, knowing we are on the way of eternal life. We know we can trust God with our departed loved ones because He is perfectly just and perfectly merciful at the same time.

> "Father in heaven, my hope for life is in You! You have helped me through the deepest hurts of life. When I am tempted to wonder if You care or even know of my troubles and sadness, I think of Jesus, who suffered more than I will ever suffer. He lived justly and was executed unjustly for my sake and for the sake of my loved ones. But He lives again! I am comforted in that hope of eternal life. Amen."

Saturday: The Vampire

Of course, I do not think there are *real* vampires, although there are many pretenders in today's world who want to be one. But the thing that fascinates me about the legend is that although this monster has a small bite, it changes the victim into a vampire also, who then finds others to victimize. There are some monstrously evil things that happen to Christians who are trying to walk the narrow way with God-love. Sorrow, anger, and disappointment brought about by offenses and injustice can create a bitter, spiteful, and vengeful person who leaves the way of God-love to become a monster to others. But there are a multitude of small injustices in life that can have the same effect on me as something "big." I fear the small bite of the vampire monster because minor stings of offence and injustice add up to nip at my soul and motivate me off of the narrow path. The Apostle Paul taught us something very important in this regard with inspired words.

> Bless the ones who persecute you. Bless and do not curse. ... Return evil for evil to no one, but think ahead of good things (to do) in front of all men. ... Do not be conquered by the evil, but conquer the evil with the good. —Romans 12:14, 17, 21

It is easy to become an angry victim of offences and injustice, real or perceived. If there are no real offences, we seem to have an ability to create them in our mind. But there is a good deal we can learn from Romans 12 that will make us "vampire-proof." There is real joy in living life like the apostle teaches us by the word of the Holy Spirit. If we will anticipate the evil actions of an enemy and do something good for them, our conscience is clear, and we see the situation as God sees it. We see the pitiful condition of the sinful human heart and thank God for His grace. We pull the fangs of the vampire. It is a preemptive defense and soothing oil for our soul.

> "Father in Heaven, help me to be one who overcomes evil with good. Save me from becoming a monster to others. Keep my heart from bitterness and desire for revenge so that I may God-love freely without hypocrisy. Make me one who never returns evil for evil but still resists the evil in this world. Help me to seek justice without vengeance. In Jesus' name, amen."

Week 5

Love Jesus

Sunday: Jesus the Way

In some cities in the world, the streets have no names. It is very difficult for someone not acquainted with the city to navigate and find a specific location. In fact, it would be impossible without direction from someone who knows the way. Jesus told His disciples that He would be going away. He said that where He was going, they could not come presently, but they would follow sometime in the future. This was very distressing to the men because they had followed Jesus faithfully for three years and had left behind families, jobs, and the futures they had planned for themselves.

> "You know the way where I go." Thomas said to Him, "Lord, we do not know where You go. How do we know the way?" Jesus said to him, "I am the way, the truth, and the life; no one comes to the Father except by Me."
> —John 14:4–6

This is fundamental to the Christian faith. Jesus is the *only way* to salvation, and His blood is the *only atonement* for our sins. That is the small gate. Following Jesus in obedience and having God-love is the *only way* to be a genuine believer in Him. Jesus said, "If you love Me, keep My commands" (John 14:15). That is the narrow path.

Many people have speculated how to walk this narrow path. Some have harshly disciplined their body to "mortify the flesh" in an effort to walk the path with integrity. Some have reasoned that it is impossible to follow the commands of Jesus and have settled on a confessional life. Some have said, "I love to sin, God loves to forgive, *so let's party!*" There is value in Christian discipline, and each of us needs the grace of God, confessing our sins, for no one is perfect. But there is a perfect way to follow Jesus on the narrow path. It is the only way. The way of God-love.

> "Father, I pray, give me a portion of Your Spirit. Your Holy Spirit ruling in me is my only hope of following on the narrow way. Forgive me, Father. I confess I have sometimes followed my own desires and passions. Make Jesus the prime desire of my soul. Increase my love for Him so that I may obey Him in all things. Help me to God-love others so I may reflect the heart of Christ. In Jesus' name, amen."

Monday: Really!

There is a question Jesus asked His disciples that I must ask myself from time to time, "Do I really have God-love for Jesus?" Jesus asked Peter this question three times without hearing back that Peter had God-love for Him, only friendly affection (John 21:15–17). Jesus asked with the God-love word (*agapé*), and Peter answered with the "I-love-you-because-you-please-me" word (*phílos*). Do I have God-love in my heart for God? It is a question Jesus directly asks those of us who say we love Him. Our love must be more than an affectionate feeling or a syrupy emotion of some kind. The syrupy sort is the kind of affection the world has for Jesus at Christmas—a lovely sentiment at a lovely time of the year. Our God-love for Jesus must also be more than admiration of His words and teachings. The test of our God-love for Jesus is simple. Do we do what He commands us to do? This is the measure Jesus uses to gauge the extent of our God-love for Him.

> If you God-love Me, you will keep My commands. ... If anyone God-loves Me, he will keep My word; and My Father will God-love him, and We will come to him and make Our home with him. He who does not God-love Me does not keep My words, and the word that you hear is not Mine but of the Father who sent Me.
> —John 14:15; 23–24

You see, we cannot truthfully claim to God-love Jesus and be a follower, believing in His words, unless we are doing what He commands. Living in obedience to the commands of Christ is a narrow road indeed. What has He commanded? That we repent of our sins, turn from darkness to light, yield ourselves to be born from above, believe that He is the Son of God, and *observe His commands to love God and to love others as ourselves.* Then we know that we God-love Jesus. We are firmly established on the narrow path.

> "Jesus, I love You. I worship You. Thank You for Your grace. Help me follow Your commands today. I pray always for Your gift of the Holy Spirit, that I may God-love You more. Fill me anew and afresh! I give myself unto You now for that purpose. Give me grace, O Jesus, that I might follow You faithfully today. Help me be Your obedient servant and faithful friend. I pray this in Your matchless name, amen."

Tuesday: The Test of God-Love

God-love compels us to make life-changing decisions. When I finally came to a place of full surrender to Christ and experienced the overflowing Spirit baptism of the love of God, the Lord reminded me of something that happened to me thirty-five years prior. At the age of nine, I received a call from God to become His minister, a preacher of the gospel. At the age of forty-four, the memory of that call still remained in my mind from mental images that were sharp, clearly understood, and compelling. I had a good job that I held for enough time to be vested in their pension. It carried a dandy 401(k) and good salary. After a year or so of trying to get into ministry, it became evident that if I was going to fulfill the call to ministry, I would have to quit.

My wife was *furious*. (I have her permission to write this. She said I could emphasize the furious part.) The church could pay little, so I bought a mower and began mowing lawns. Space does not permit me to write a memoir, but in my seventy-third year of life, I want to testify that God loves us with God-love and supplies every need and more. I now realize that I gave up nothing to follow the will of God and gained *everything*. The Apostle Peter came to such a life-changing God-love decision. The risen Lord Jesus came to Peter along the Sea of Galilee to call him once again to be a shepherd of the church. Peter had returned to commercial fishing, the job he knew best.

> Then when they had finished a meal of fish, Jesus said, "Simon, son of Jonah, do you God-love Me more than these (fish)?" Simon said, "Lord, you know that I have affection (human-love) for you." Jesus said, "Feed my lambs." —John 21:15

Twice more Jesus asked Peter the God-love question. Twice more Simon Peter answered that he had human-love for Jesus. Jesus commanded Peter each time to be the spiritual leader and become Christ's pastor of the church. Scripture does not record when the final collapse of Peter's self-will occurred. I believe it happened at Pentecost when the Spirit fell on them with power and a gushing out of God-love. Peter's call is not my call. My call is not your call. Each one has a different life to live for Jesus. But God-love in our hearts for Jesus will keep us in His will on the straight and narrow path.

> "Jesus, I will love You with God-love today. Keep me on the narrow path of obedience to Your commands *and* Your call. Amen."

Wednesday: Born

I guess there are some people who, when they are in times of great distress, wish they had never been born. I do not fault them for that because I have not experienced their level of misery. But I have never felt that way. I like living and try to enjoy as much of it as possible. Memories of good and bad times, of safety and danger, of health and illness, of youth and old age flood my mind as I write. Yet I cannot say that I wish I had never been born. But there is a price for being born that will take me beyond the day-by-day experiences of humanity. Life comes to an end for everyone who is born. I fear death because God put that within every creature. But in Christ I have no terror of it. That is one of the reasons I love Jesus. When He was *born*, the immortal Eternal Word took on mortality to share the experience of death with us. He committed Himself to death so that we may someday exchange our mortal body for an immortal one. In Him we no longer need to be terrorized by the idea of our own death.

> For if by the trespass of one man, death ruled ... so life will rule by the one man, Jesus Christ. —Romans 5:17

Jesus appeared from the womb of a woman just as each of us did when we made our entrance into life. He had the human experiences of life. Jesus loved His family, enjoyed friends and good food, laughed and grieved with people, was disrespected by family, betrayed by a friend, lied about, falsely accused, and tortured to death. He cried out with loud cries, face down in the darkness of the garden, agonizing over His forthcoming sacrifice. All of this because He was *born* of God and woman so that we could live forever in the next life: *God-love*. We have to God-love Him for that!

"Thank You, Lord, for eternal life. Jesus has provided the way; may I walk in that way all my life. Forgive me, Lord, for any thought that I may have had that You do not care about me. Help me always to remember that Jesus was *born* for the sake of sinners like me. Amen."

Thursday: Friends

When I came to repentance, I can honestly say I did not have a friend. I had plenty of acquaintances and some people I hung out with, but I didn't have anyone I could count on in a pinch. To tell the truth, the greater part of the problem was that I was not much of a friend to anyone. When the personal transformation of grace began, I started to learn how to be a true friend. In Christ I found friends, people I could count on in a crisis, people with whom I share my inmost thoughts. I try to be the same kind of a friend to them. I love Jesus because He is the most wonderful of friends. He taught us to God-love each other in the same way He loves us.

> This is my command, that you God-love one another as I have God-loved you. No one has greater God-love than this, that someone would lay down his life for his friends. You are friends of Mine if you do what I command. I do not call you slaves any longer, because the servant does not know what his Lord does. But you I have called friends because I have made known everything that I heard from My Father. —John 15:12–15

When we God-love like that it is easy to find friends. Each of the people Jesus was talking to in this passage were not as good a friend to Jesus as He was to them. In a few hours, all of them would betray Him, and Jesus knew it. True God-love gives to others without expecting the same level of love. By His example, Jesus taught us that if we want to have friends we have to cut them some slack. When we try to be the better part of a friendship, we are like Jesus. In Jesus we find the perfect friend who is always the better part of our friendship.

"Lord Jesus, thank You for being my friend. You have given everything to me, beginning with my life. I want to be a better friend to You and keep your commands. Bless me that I may God-love others as You have loved me. Give me grace, Lord, that I may receive love from others as I have received God-love from You. Keep me on the straight and narrow. Amen."

Friday: Finding Jesus

One of the great adventures I have had was a visit to Israel a few years ago. The people I traveled with invited me to add a place to the itinerary, so I requested that we visit Sepphoris, the capital city of Galilee in the time of Jesus. Located on a hill across a valley from Nazareth Village, it is now an archeological site. Herod Antipas built the city during the years when Jesus was maturing with His family in Nazareth. Taking decades and more than a thousand craftsmen to build, Josephus called the city the "ornament of all Galilee." It reportedly had many shops along its broad market street. It is so near the hometown of Jesus that I think, along with others, that Joseph and Jesus found work there as *tekton,* workers in wood. As I stood at the place of the palace of Herod Antipas, I looked across the valley to Nazareth. I thought of how Herod sent out his agents to seek for Jesus and could not find Him. Yet Jesus had been near to him for years, possibly involved in building the very home the king lived in. For he, like his father Herod the Great, only sought for Jesus that he might kill Him.

> Some Pharisees approached saying to Him (Jesus), "Get out of here, for Herod wishes to kill You" ... He said to them, "Tell that fox, look! I cast out demons and perform healings today and tomorrow, and on the third day I will be finished ... You will not see Me until you can say, 'Blessed is He who comes in the name of the Lord.'" —Luke 13:31–32, 35

To find God we must find Jesus. Jesus told us that we must love Him and bless Him before we may find Him. To love Jesus is to confess our sins, embrace His Cross, and bless *Him* for the sacrifice that saves our soul. If we follow His commands, we *prove* our God-love toward Jesus. And what are His commands? Obey Him and do unto others as we would have done unto ourselves.

> "Father in Heaven, how blessed is Jesus who came in Your name. He truly is full of grace and truth. Help me, Lord, to be obedient to God-love and assist me that I may love in sincerity and truth. Show me the unloving ways in my heart, and lead me in the narrow path. Amen."

Saturday: Come Follow Me

There is a universal command that Jesus gives to all who wish to have eternal life, "Come follow Me." It is an invitation to those who love Jesus to submit their own will to the will of God and follow Him along the path of God-love. Sometimes this requires a drastic change in our lifestyle, aspirations, and goals. Soon after I began the journey along the narrow way with Jesus, I attended a trade association rubber-chicken-dinner for my company. It was a merry, noisy affair with talk of sales and deals that could be made and all kinds of business conversations, lubricated liberally with refreshments. In the past I had joined right in, but this evening was different. All during the affair I felt detached from the noise and conversation of commerce. I heard in my mind's ear the call of Jesus, "Follow Me." It was the same kind of thing that happened to Simon Peter when Jesus took him on a walk down the shore and asked him three times, "Do you God-love Me more than your business of fishing?"

> Turning about, Peter saw the disciple Jesus loved following them. This was the same one who reclined at the table next to Jesus and said, "Who is the one betraying You?" Having seen him, Peter said, "What about this one?" Jesus said to him, "If I wish for him to remain until I come, what is that to you? You follow Me!" —John 21:20–22

That disciple Jesus loved was the Lord's close relative (the son of Mary's sister Salome) and probably not much more than thirteen years of age. When we God-love Jesus we keep our eyes upon Him and what He wants for us. We cease worrying about what God may or may not do for others. Jesus may want us to remain godly in the "fishing business," or perhaps there is another career path or occupation. God-love places all that in the hands and will of God. When we love Him like that, our life begins to conform to His, and our needs are met in Him. God-love takes self from the throne of our life and seats Jesus as our Master and King.

> "Jesus, I will follow You. I trust You with my life. Give me direction, and fill me with the knowledge of Your will. May Your will be done in me today. Amen."

Week 6

Love Others

Sunday: The First Rule of God-Love

Rules are good when God-love rules. I am generally against excessive rules in religion that go beyond the laws plainly laid out by Jesus and the apostles and the Ten Commandments. But there must be rules to define how we keep the law and govern the flow of human activity. Imagine the chaos and carnage on our streets and highways without rules of the road.

But rules in religion have often been used to enforce conformity to a norm that is more severe than what the Bible teaches. Legalism can suck the joy right out of being a follower of Jesus Christ. Legalism says that we become holy by conforming to a strict set of rules and by doing holy things. But Jesus and His apostles taught us that we become holy through *grace* and the *transforming power* of God-love given to us by the Holy Spirit. Jesus' rules for us are all about God-love. The Apostle Paul explained it.

> Owe nothing to anyone except to God-love one another; for the one who loves the other has fulfilled the law. For, "You shall not commit adultery, you shall not murder, you shall not steal, you shall not covet," and if there is any other commandment, it is summed up in this word, "You shall God-love your neighbor as yourself." God-love does no evil to a neighbor; therefore, God-love fulfills the law. —Romans 13:8–10

So the first rule on the narrow path of God-love toward others is "do no harm." We do not want to think of ourselves as harmless, especially the men. It carries an implication of weakness. But if we think of it as doing no evil, we understand the way God-love works. If we think we love a person who is the spouse of another and are tempted to commit adultery, God-love tells us

82

that if we truly love that person, we will not drag them into sin and ultimately into the judgment of God. If we truly God-love others we will not murder, steal, or even have the strong desire to have the things that belong to our neighbor. God-love never fails. Through God-love we become harmless to others.

> "Father in Heaven, I pray that You would make me harmless to every human being. Help me to understand where I must be strong to defend myself and others. But help me never to be the source of evil and always be just in Your sight. May I never return evil for evil but always do unto others as I would have done to myself. Amen."

Monday: Positive and Negative

Jesus gave the mechanism for loving others in His command, "Therefore, everything that you wish men do to you, do you also to them. For this is the law and the prophets" (Matthew 7:12). This rule is found in all of the major religions of the world. Most state the same thing, though in a negative way. Confucius said, "Do not do to others what you do not want done to yourself." Jesus states this universal ethic of reciprocity in a positive way so that God-love not only refrains one from evil action, but it spurs us to good positive action toward others. The apostles continued in this teaching in their words and deeds. Doing good was Jesus' occupation on His way to the Cross. When at the command of the Lord, Peter went to the home of the Roman centurion Cornelius to preach the gospel, he assumed the Gentiles understood who Jesus was and the good He did.

> You know the thing that came to be in all Judea ... How the One from Nazareth, Jesus, was anointed by God with the Holy Spirit and power. He went about doing good and healing all those who were oppressed by the devil, because God was with Him. —Acts 10:37–38

We see the positive way Jesus put His rule into practice. In God-love, He went out to the masses and did what was good for people. This is what many people think makes a person a Christian and a "good person." Whatever good Jesus did for the people of His community was because of what He was as a *person*. The Holy Spirit was all over Jesus, and the divine God-love spilled out of Him in righteous and holy action toward others. Likewise, when we surrender our will to the will of God and ask Him for the Holy Spirit (Luke 11:13), God lavishes His God-love upon us (Romans 5:5), and we become a reflection of the One who "went about doing good."

"Father in Heaven, I beg of You to give me what Jesus promised—the Holy Spirit. Anoint me with God-love so I may be a reflection of Jesus, no matter how imperfect that may be. Help me to see the hidden need of others. Open my eyes to the good I might do so I may be like Jesus, who went about doing good. Amen."

Tuesday: The Lighted Way

It was a dark night and a dark road. A California fog was settling in on Pfeiffer Big Sur State Park, and my teen group from church was stumbling down a dark road. We were on a sponsored outing and had decided to walk a distance from our camp to a store to buy some snacks. It was dusk when we left and a very pleasant day. By the time we decided to return, it was turning dark, and a California fog had descended. Soon we could not see our hands in front of our faces. No streetlights lined the road and, of course, no one thought to bring a flashlight. Cell phones were a thing of science fiction at the time, and we were in trouble. We clung to each other and felt the way with our feet. Laughing and worrying at the same time, we called out our names to make sure no one got separated. Occasionally a car would come along, and we could see the road ahead for a moment and then back into darkness. We eventually made it unharmed to camp and soon forgot the fun and terror of that evening. Jesus is the light that illumines the narrow path of God-love. His teachings are brilliant lamps to show the way. But we also light the way for ourselves and others when we faithfully follow His commands. Jesus said something astounding about us who have sought the small gate and are trying to walk the narrow path of God-love.

> You are the light of the world, a city laid upon a hill cannot be hidden, nor does anyone light a lamp and put it under a bushel basket but puts it on a lampstand so that it is light for everyone in the house. In the same way, let your light shine in front of all people so they will see your good works and glorify your Father in the heavens. —Matthew 5:14–16

We illumine the narrow way of God-love and are illuminated by others who walk with love. We need to love and be loved. When people see the followers of Jesus acting out with God-love, it speaks to their heart and helps draw them out of darkness to the light of Jesus Christ. Perhaps He will lead them to the small gate and they will walk the narrow path as a brother or sister.

> "Lord, give me Your God-love today so I may illumine the path for others on the way. Use me to God-love those who do not walk the path in such a way that it honors and reveals Jesus Christ and His grace to them. In Jesus' name, amen."

Wednesday: The Rainbow Man

The Rainbow Man was once one of the most recognizable people in America. During the seventies and eighties we saw him on television at all kinds of sporting events. He topped his head with a rainbow-colored wig and held up a sign that said, "JOHN 3:16." He wore a T-shirt that boldly said, "Believe in Jesus Christ." Somehow he managed to get into just about every major sporting event in America. We saw him behind the goal at the NBA finals, at NFL playoff games, at World Series baseball games, even behind the pit wall of the Indianapolis 500 winner. The message he proclaimed from John 3:16 was wonderful, "For God so God-loved the *world*, that He gave His only begotten Son, that whoever believes in Him shall not perish, but have eternal life" (author's emphasis). The Rainbow Man claimed to be "born again," which is the message of Jesus. But somehow, the Rainbow Man did not get the whole idea of God-love. He got into a lot of trouble, becoming very violent and abusive. He started being disruptive at sporting events, setting off stink bombs, and ended up kidnapping a woman and threatening to shoot at airplanes around LAX airport in Los Angeles. Finally, he was given three consecutive life sentences for kidnapping the woman and numerous other violent acts.

> Beloved, let us God-love one another, because God-love is from God and everyone who God-loves God has been born of God and knows God. The one who does not God-love does not know God because God is God-love. —1 John 4:7–8

If we accept the inspired words of the Apostle John, we understand it is not possible to walk the straight and narrow path without God-love, without words and deeds that show the message of John 3:16. It is not enough to claim we have God-love. We must live it out in relationship to God and to others. We can proclaim the gospel to the whole world and reach millions of people just like the Rainbow Man. But if we do not have God-love, we are less than nothing.

> "Father in heaven, forgive me where I have forgotten Your message to me in Jesus Christ. May I God-love others in the same manner You have loved me. I want to know You, God. May I always seek to follow the path of God-love. Help me to repair any damage I may have done to others, and help me to right actions toward others today. In Jesus' name, amen."

Thursday: The Virtues of God-Love

The Christian faith is all about relationship, being in right relationship with God and others. Grace and faith put me in right relationship with God, and God-love places me in right relationship to others. God-love can make me a good husband, a good dad, a good pastor, and a good neighbor if I will walk by the Holy Spirit. He teaches me to God-love and continually develops the virtues of God-love in me. It keeps me on the straight and narrow. The more I obey Jesus and do unto others as I would have done to me, the better my relationship with both God and people. The less I God-love, the worse my relationship. The Apostle Paul wrote to the people of Corinth to tell them that everything they were doing for the Lord had to be done in God-love, and every giftedness they believed they possessed was nothing without it. He described God-love by the virtues it brings forth.

> God-love is patient, is kind; God-love is not envious, does not brag, is not puffed up, is not indecent, does not seek things selfishly, is not provoked to anger, does not keep a log of evil deeds, does not applaud injustice; God-love rejoices with the truth. —1 Corinthians 13:4–6

This passage of Scripture should prompt each of us to prayer because we cannot claim to conform perfectly to this standard of God-love. Perhaps I should just speak for myself. But my experience as a pastor teaches me that we all have room to grow. This text from 1 Corinthians is a good passage to pray at the end of the day when we are preparing for sleep. When I ask the Lord about how I did with God-love, He always answers honestly and with grace.

"Lord, have I shown patience with people today? Have I shown kindness in being helpful to someone today? Have I shown God-love in obedience to You? Have I been braggadocious and overbearing today? Am I embarrassed by some indecency that occurred today? Was I selfish today? Did I remain calm, or did I let somebody get under my skin? Did I add to the list of wrongs of others toward me so that I have another thing that keeps me from sleep? Did I cheer when someone I admire lied about someone I do not care for? Did I rejoice with the truth even when it put me at a disadvantage? Lord, I need more of Your God-love. Forgive me where I have fallen short. Bring forth in me the virtues of God-love. Amen."

Friday: The Requirements of God

My parents were overjoyed when I called to tell them I had come to repentance. They never lost hope that Jesus would save their lost boy. With faith in God, Mom prayed for me every day from the time she knew she had conceived until her death at age ninety-two. Except for Jesus, she knew me better than any other human being; no one God-loved me more.

A few weeks after I made my announcement to them, Mom called to see how I was doing. I thought I was doing great, and every day seemed filled with the glory of God. But the words from my mother went something like, "Buddy (my nickname), I know you. You do everything like you are killing snakes. There is a Scripture I want you to look up, Micah chapter six. I want to talk to you about it." She waited until I could get my Bible and find Micah, which is a hard book to find if you are not real acquainted with the Bible because he is a Minor Prophet (only minor because the book is short and harder to find than the big boys like Isaiah and Jeremiah). When I got back to the phone, she read it to me.

> With what shall I come to the LORD and bow myself before the God on high? ... He has told you, O man, what is good; and what does the Lord require of you but to do justice, to love kindness, and to walk humbly with your God? —Micah 6:6, 8 NASB

It was one of the best sermons I have ever received. Mom told me I do not have to set the world on fire for Jesus. Rather, I needed to submit my will to the will of God and humbly try to do that will, acting justly and with mercy toward everyone.

There it is! Love God supremely and God-love others sincerely. It changed my concept of what it means to be a Christian. When we live out God-love toward others we do His will and fulfill His requirements for us.

> "Father God, thank You for the insight I received from Your Word through my mom. Thank You for the grace You gave to her and the Holy Spirit that made her a wise and loving person. Help me that I may live by the words of the prophet to act with justice and mercy toward others and walk humbly with You for all of my days. Amen."

Saturday: The Good Shepherd

My wife and I have owned several Chihuahuas over the years. One time we took a beautiful long-haired Chihuahua with us when we went to visit my sister and brother-in-law who had a couple of nice shelties, who are herding dogs. We brought a small kennel for our dog so she would have a safe place. We put the small dog on the floor to test how the bigger dogs would get along with her. After things went peacefully, we let them interact freely. That is when the sheltie instinct began to emerge. They began herding the reluctant small dog out of the living area, down the hall, into the guest bedroom and into her kennel. Then they lay down in front of the kennel to keep the small dog "safe." We got a good laugh out of that and a good lesson. With God-love, Jesus has a shepherding instinct for us and constantly works to keep us safe.

> I am the Good Shepherd, and I know My own and my own know Me. Just as the Father knows Me and I know the Father, so My life I lay down for the sheep.
> —John 10:14–15

If we follow the example of the Good Shepherd, we will discover a shepherding instinct in being His follower. How much joy there is when we find a fellowship where we can imitate Jesus in this way! The church should be a place where mutual shepherding takes place with all the saints looking out for each other, placing the safety of others above their own. Where is such a church? It is in the same place we can find the perfect church. It cannot be found in perfect form. But we can work to create such a culture as much as God can help us to do so. Many acts of kindness and helpfulness will not be reciprocated, but we should persist in

God-love without bitterness or recrimination. Imitate Jesus, for He loves the world when for the most part, the world will not God-love Him back.

> "Jesus, I know You are the Good Shepherd because that is the way You treated me. You came looking for me. Help me to imitate Your example, so I can be a shepherd to my brothers and sisters today. Give me the grace to humbly receive shepherding from others so that they may be blessed by extending God-love to me. Amen."

Week 7

You Gotta Love 'em

Sunday: Tough Love

When I think of tough love, I think of giving an ultimatum to someone who needs it in order to make a good decision about the direction of their life and the condition of their character. That is something that must be done with prayer, great forethought, and God-love. I think, however, that the toughest of all love is to God-love someone who has harmed me, to God-love my enemy.

Once I had a coworker who was very ambitious and thought I was some kind of obstacle on his ladder to success. When I was absent from a managers' meeting because I was supervising in the field, he would trash-talk and lie about me. The other people would tell me, "George, you gotta *do* something." I generally believe in defending myself against physical assaults and lies, but something in my heart told me to let God fight this battle for me. "You're crazy," the others told me.

Finally, the man sabotaged some equipment I was using, and I narrowly escaped disaster. When Jesus told me to do something good for my worst enemy, I decided to try it and see what would happen. At the next managers' meeting the man told the group he was moving his elderly father to a retirement community. I asked if he could use some help. On our next day off, I helped him move furniture and boxes to a storage facility. We never became friends, but the war ended. Thank You, Jesus.

> You have heard it said, you shall God-love your neighbor and hate your enemy. But I say to you God-love your enemies, and pray for those who are persecuting you so that you may become the sons of your Father in the heavens who causes His sun to rise upon the evil and the good and rains upon the just and the unjust. ... You will be perfect, therefore, as your Heavenly Father is perfect. —Matthew 5:43–48

The only possibility of human perfection that can be discovered in the teachings of Jesus or His apostles is found in God-love for God and for others. That includes our enemies, those who harm us. It is at the top of the list of moral dilemmas each Christian will face in life. Place Jesus' teaching in this matter to the test. Pray for your worst enemy, and try to do something good for them, whether they will receive it or not. God will help.

> "Father in Heaven, I am thinking of someone right now, an enemy I have to deal with. Help me to God-love them and find something good to do for them. This is difficult, but I have faith You will help me. Amen."

Monday: Detractors

I like to be liked. Don't we all? I want people to think well of me. The approval by people of what I do and what I say is important to me. But, as followers of Jesus Christ, we understand there is a satanic force of evil in this world. Being the father of lies, Satan works at all times to destroy our credibility in the culture. As a result, we find that many people hate us simply because we follow Jesus and call ourselves Christian.

In the media and in entertainment, we are depicted as the most horrible and radical of people. In the arts, they mock and marginalize us, showing disgusting pictures of our crucified Lord, depicting Mary as an immoral woman, and proposing many false depictions of Christians. Academia exalts heretical writers, promoting misinformation and slander of all kinds. I just saw a headline from media that calls itself "history" that asked the question, "Did George Washington Believe in God?" The author thought President Washington was "cagey" about religion. Really? They should read his speeches and his journal and the eyewitness accounts of his contemporaries!

It seems like there is a lot of sensitivity shown to all kinds of religions except Christianity. Concerning us, anything goes. Jesus prophesied that this would happen.

> Blessed-happy are you when men hate you, and exclude you, and revile you, and throw out your name as evil, for the sake of the Son of Man. Rejoice in that day and jump for joy, for look, your reward in heaven is great! —Luke 6:22–23

That's just the way it is. We cannot say that Jesus hid these things from us. These things that He prophesied that would happen to us were the very things that happened to Him. It is our opportunity to imitate our Savior, to show God-love and not hate back, to not revile them, to never return evil for evil and to pray for them. That is what Jesus did, and He said that no servant is greater than his master. Our Master is Jesus the Good Shepherd, who turned His back to derision and ignored insults. We are blessed-happy when we do the same.

> "Father in heaven, the words people say about me and others who follow Jesus Christ are just that: words. Truth resides in Jesus. If I have faith in Jesus Christ and follow His example, insults and derision have no effect on me. No one can do anything to me to take away the eternal life Jesus Christ gave me. Thank You, Lord Jesus. Amen."

Tuesday: The Boss

One of the most difficult situations in which to show God-love to others is when one is the boss, a person who is in authority over others. When people do their job and business is good and there are profits to show, there is seldom difficulty. But when I have had to supervise a problem employee or an employee with a problem they will not address, the straight and narrow gets a little rocky. More often, the test of God-love in my life is how I deal with my boss. How do I treat the one in authority over me? Sometimes we have to fire and get fired.

The Christians in the early church faced a unique problem in this regard. Masters and slaves called each other brother and sister. They had been called into a fellowship of God-love that "treated others as they would be treated." Nothing could be changed about the culture of master/slave authority because of the Roman government. In the same way, we have little alternative to dealing with the boss/employee relationships where we work. The Apostle Paul addressed this problem in several places in his inspired writing.

> In all things, in whatever you do in word or work, do it all in the name of the Lord Jesus Christ, giving thanks to God the Father through Him. —Colossians 3:17

> Masters, give justice and equality to your slaves, knowing that you also have a Master in heaven. —Colossians 4:1

> Those (slaves) having believers as masters must not be disrespectful to them; because they are brothers, and must serve them better, because those who get

> the benefit of your good work are believers and God-loved. —1 Timothy 6:2

These principles apply to Christians trying to walk the straight and narrow as free people who are always under authority and sometimes have authority over others. If bosses and employees both will stand in each other's shoes and God-love one another, we will treat each other with fairness and respect, and we will stay on the path of God-love. Both boss and worker will become more productive and valuable in the economy and so benefit the whole nation. Then we can all receive our pay with integrity and a good conscience. So much as it is up to us, let there be peace and God-love in the world.

> "Lord, help me as I work today. Strengthen my mind and my hands for work. Help me to give my best effort so I may always have a good conscience. May God-love rule my deeds and words today. I dedicate everything I say and do today to You, Lord Jesus Christ. Amen."

Wednesday: Weighing God-Love

I have a lot of appreciation for those men and women who work for us in law enforcement, especially the Christians who try to follow Jesus in that difficult occupation. I served as a chaplain on a police force for several years. Often, when I was riding on patrol with officers, this question would come up, "How can I justify shooting anyone?" Having to use lethal force in the course of duty is the worst nightmare for an officer tying to follow Jesus Christ with God-love. They must make quick decisions and are trained to instantly recognize deadly situations. Police shootings average a three-foot distance, three shots, and three seconds. An officer can only act to kill if their life or the life of another innocent person is in peril, or in a few other specific instances. If they hesitate or act impulsively, they may end up dead or in prison. They will have to justify their actions by answering two questions, "Why did you start shooting; why did you stop?" But the most important answer is the one the officer must give to God. There is a Scripture passage that I consistently talked about when an officer brought up this question.

> Rulers are not a terror to those who do good deeds but to those who do evil ... for he is a servant of God to you for good. But if you do evil, fear; he does not carry the sword for nothing. —Romans 13:3–4

We, like the officers, must constantly weigh God-love. Our lives do not belong to us but to God. We are charged with protecting our life and the lives of others. We must carefully consider the God-love we have toward our family and brothers and sisters and weigh that against any God-love we have toward those who would harm them. The good must outweigh the evil. In God-love, we must guard our lives and the lives of the innocent using whatever force is necessary against violent people.

"Lord, I praise You for Your grace toward me. Thank You for providing me with the means to defend myself, my family, my brothers and sisters in the fellowship, and every innocent person against evil people. I pray that will never be necessary. Thank You for the police and all those who do what they are able to protect us and to stop evildoers. Give me the wisdom of God-love and discernment in the moment. Amen."

Thursday: Rapport

I once attended a seminar conducted by a negotiator for law enforcement. He was the one who talked to people who were armed and barricaded or who were holding hostages in an effort to get them to surrender peacefully with no harm to anyone, including themselves. He said the first thing that is necessary in such a case is to establish *rapport*, which means a relationship characterized by agreement, mutual understanding, or empathy that makes communication possible or easy. To illustrate, he gave us an acrostic.

Respect
Another
Person's
Perspective
Obtain
Respect (and)
Trust
    Louis "Geno" Dorough
    Compliant Surrender

How can we be at peace with those who seem to always oppose us and insist on being an enemy? How can we begin to get along with the people with whom our personalities seem to clash? Sometimes there is no right or wrong, but some people just don't like us, and we have mutual feelings. Perhaps we are in the wrong. The beginning of the solution is to respect the other person's perspective, to "put the shoe on the other foot."

> Speak well to the ones persecuting you; speak well and do not curse. Rejoice with those who rejoice; weep with those who weep. Think the same thing to one another, not lofty thoughts, but be led away to the

106

> lowly; do not become wise in yourself. Return evil for evil to no one. Think ahead of good things to do before all people. If possible, for you, live in peace with all men. ... Do not be conquered with evil but conquer evil with good. —Romans 12:14–18; 21

If we try to view things from other people's perspectives it will help us in every relationship we have and will facilitate some kind of accommodation with others. Often, it will enable us to see the needs of the one who troubles us and give us an opportunity to do something good for them. It will not be possible to be at peace with everyone at all times. But God-love makes the effort and gives us joy that comes from a clear conscience and perhaps a new friend, brother, or sister in the Lord.

> "Jesus, help me to God-love others as You have loved me. When I was contrary, You came to me with mercy, grace, and forgiveness. You call me friend whom I once treated as an enemy. I worship You, Lord, and I will always follow You down the narrow path. Amen."

Friday: Politicians

Politics can eclipse everything we think is right and wrong. Perhaps I should speak for myself, but I do not think I am alone. I have those politicians and leaders I like and respect because of their philosophy of governing and their ability to lead. I have others I do not care for at all. When there is a leader I like, it is easy to pray for them, speak well of them, and be filled with God-love for them. I confess, if the leader is not one I respect, it is difficult to say anything good about them or pray for them at all.

There are plenty of voices in the media and elsewhere telling me whom to support. They rejoice in every success and excuse every failure of their favorite. Their perspective is that Jesus would clearly vote for the persons they promote. In my lifetime, the leaders I like or do not like have been split about half and half. So the challenge of God-love has been great. The utmost help to me has been to pray sincerely for every leader and politician that God would bless them with mercy and grace and protect them and their families from harm.

> Therefore, I admonish, first of all, requests, prayers, intercessions, and thanksgivings to be made on behalf of all people, on behalf of kings and all those who are in authority, that we may lead a peaceful and quiet life in all godliness and reverence. —1 Timothy 2:1–2

The king Paul referred to was none other than Nero, the Emperor of Rome. By almost all accounts Nero was a vile and malignant narcissist who burned Rome and blamed it on the Christians. He is the same king who ordered the Apostle Paul beheaded on the Appian way. It would be easy to blaspheme and hate a leader such as Nero. First-century theologian John Chrysostom preached on this Scripture, "No one can feel hatred toward those for whom he prays" (Homilies on 1 Timothy). The people of that day had no say about who would be emperor. We, in our free democracies, do have a say with our voice and our vote, being able to praise or criticize our leaders freely. God-love will praise and criticize but never revile or lie.

> "Lord, I pray for my leaders at this hour. Keep them healthy and safe; preserve their life and the life of their family. Help my leader, Lord, to make good decisions to protect our freedom and safety. May they strengthen justice and love mercy. Bring good counselors around them. May Your grace be upon my leader. In Jesus' name, amen."

Saturday: Motorists

"If someone takes from thee the right lane, give unto them the left lane also." This is the motto I have for driving calmly and defensively. I generally do that, but it is hard for me to find any God-love in it. Jesus said we could be in big trouble if we call anyone "you fool" (Matthew 5:22). In the Bible, the Greek word for "fool" is *móros:* moron. I hope Jesus meant speaking face-to-face with a fool and not from the inside of a car with the windows rolled up. When some ... moron-person comes flying along the interstate in heavy traffic, weaving in and out, missing cars by the narrowest of margins, it is hard not to yell at them. Or if I see some person putting on makeup while in rush hour traffic or texting, I have bad thoughts. Such motorists definitely disturb my peace and cause me to question my God-love. I try not to stare at them as they speed past. I guess I could say something like Mom used to say, "Oh, for pity's sake!"

> He who restrains his words has knowledge, and he who has a cool spirit is a man of understanding. Even a fool, when he keeps silent, is considered wise; when he closes his lips, he is considered prudent. — Proverbs 17:27–28 NASB

The best policy when driving is to have "a cool spirit" when a maniac is risking his or her life on the road and jeopardizing others also. The first thing to remember is that when one remains calm and cool in an emergency, it might mean the difference between a near miss and a disaster. God-love thinks of protecting the life of that nut because God loves them too, and perhaps if we could understand their state of mind or their lost condition, we could exert God-love to them. Perhaps we would even pray for them as their taillights go quickly out of sight. Then we would not only *walk* the straight and narrow, we would *drive* it also.

> "Father in heaven, I need Your help to keep a cool spirit while I drive. Give me calmness and a sure hand on the wheel that I may preserve my life and the life of others on the road. Give me of Your spirit of God-love that I may have peace of mind and never use abusive language or name-call, even in the isolation of my vehicle. Then I will speak and act as one wise and not foolish. In Jesus' name, amen."

Week 8

The Paideia of the Father

Sunday: Paideia

The New Testament was originally written in a language called Koine Hellenistic, common Greek. It was established three hundred years prior to Jesus by Alexander the Great to try to change the culture of the nations he conquered to reflect the Greek model. By the time of the New Testament it had become nearly everyone's second language. It is also the language of the Septuagint, the Greek translation of the Hebrew Scriptures (Old Testament), that the New Testament writers quoted word for word.

All this to say, I have found the study of the words of the Greek New Testament to be very helpful in understanding what the writers were trying to communicate. Some Greek words carry concepts that teach us something about walking along the straight and narrow. The concept of this book is about the word *agape, God-love.* The Greek word *paideia* is often translated "discipline," but it also carries the concept of education and training. With God-love, the Father has placed each of us in His *paideia* school.

> We had human fathers and teachers we respected; how much more should we be submissive to the Father of spirits and live? For they disciplined (*paideia*) us for a few days according to what seemed right to them; but He for our benefit. All discipline (*paideia*) does not seem to be joyful but grievous. But to the ones having been trained by it, it pays off in righteousness. —Hebrews 12:9–11

The Greek idea was that the father had the responsibility to raise his children to be responsible citizens in their democratic societies. They were under his *paideia*; he taught and trained them, disciplined them with reward and punishment, and provided tutors until he was satisfied that they were prepared for adulthood. This is how God loves us. He takes us to school, not for a few days, but for our entire life. He does not want us to remain infants in the faith knowing little of God-love, stumbling down the straight and narrow, losing our way, and falling into the ditch. He wants us to be godly, to live with God-love according to His command.

> "Righteous Father, I submit myself to Your *paideia*. Teach me God-love, Lord, and discipline me as seems right to You. I know it is for my benefit. Lead me in the paths of righteousness for Your sake. Make me fit for Your kingdom, loving You supremely and others sincerely. Amen."

Monday: True Child

My Dad was a stern man in a lot of ways, but I never doubted his love for me. He never disciplined me because of anger, although I made him plenty angry with my behavior and determination to be a slacker. Sometimes he applied the APPY BIRTHDAY paddle to my posterior. The paddle had been inherited, probably from *his* father, and originally read HAPPY BIRTHDAY, but the H had been worn off with use. The paddle was always applied for my good and justly; I deserved every whack. He always taught me and urged me to be a better person, to achieve more and to be responsible. Receiving his discipline, I was receiving his God-love for me. When I became an adult, he treated me like one and respected my decisions in life even though he did not agree with some of them. I miss his godly counsel and practical advice. He always knew what to do. I have never questioned that he was my father and I his son.

> You have forgotten the exhortation He (the Father) spoke to you, "My Son, do not dismiss the discipline (*paideia*) of the Lord, and do not faint when rebuked by Him; for those whom the Lord loves, He disciplines and flogs every son He receives." Because of discipline you endure. God deals with you as sons; for what son does the Father not discipline? But if you are without discipline, of which all have partaken, then you are bastards and not sons. —Hebrews 12:5–8

When the Holy Spirit is scourging our mind and soul for some failure, we tend to become discouraged. But the Bible says we should not be disheartened and totally crushed down with guilt or remorse. Instead we should be encouraged by the God-love coming our way and learn to love more that we may be better sons and daughters of our Father in heaven. We should receive the instructions of the Bible with the guidance of the Spirit. If we have harmed someone, ask for forgiveness, and try to make amends. If we have sinned against God, we must ask for forgiveness and grace that we may avoid future transgression. Receive the *paideia* of the Father, for He has received you as His very own child.

> "Thank You, Father, for receiving me as a true child. Teach me Your ways; instruct me on the straight and narrow way of God-love. Your rebuke is better than all the praise of the world. Amen."

Tuesday: Gifts from the Father

There is a great desire among many in the church to be the recipient of gifts from the Father. The gift that *every* Christian has is the gift of His *grace*, without which no one can be saved. But the Bible also teaches us that spiritual gifts are disbursed among the Father's children as He sees fit, giving abilities so we may build His kingdom.

The desire among the saints for spiritual powers is as old as the church. The members of the New Testament church of Corinth eagerly sought these abilities that seemed to make them *special*. The Apostle Paul listed them as wisdom, knowledge, faith, healing, miracles, prophecy, spiritual discernment, tongues, and interpretation of tongues. Paul asserted that each member had a gift, but no one had all the gifts, and each saint was gifted differently: "All these are the work of the One and same Spirit, apportioning to each person individually as He wishes" (1 Corinthians 12:11). Some of the people of the Corinthian church had become disdainful of the spiritual abilities of others and overly proud of their own. The apostle admonished them and wrote that they should ask the Father for the greatest gift and so receive an ability of incomparable spiritual power.

> You zealously desire the greater gifts. Yet I will show you an incomparably better way. If I speak in the languages of men and of angels but do not have God-love, I have become a loud gong or a crashing cymbal. If I have prophecy and understand all the mysteries and all knowledge, and if I have faith to move mountains but have not God-love, I am nothing. —1 Corinthians 12:31—13:2

118

Through the people of Corinth, Paul tells us that if we knew the languages of the mission fields so that we could interpret for a preacher, or if we could speak and understand the tongues of angels, or could interpret any spiritual language, or if we could preach like Billy Graham, or if we memorized the Bible backwards in Greek, but we do not have God-love, we are nothing but a bunch of wind and noise. He goes on to say even if we are martyred and have not God-love, there is no profit in it for us (1 Corinthians 13:3). God has better ministry for us than we can imagine, but all success depends on God-love.

> "Oh Father, give me a better perspective of what it means to be a Christian. Give me a better view of ministry and the gifts and resources that You have given me. Increase my God-love for You and others, I pray. Amen."

Wednesday: The First Beneficiary

The most difficult lessons to learn in the schoolhouse of the Lord have to do with loving others. Someone has said that there is a God-shaped hole in our heart that can only be filled by Him and His grace. I know that is true because when I ached for God to be a part of my life, His grace was sufficient to fill that void and gave me joy and peace. But I had no such hole in my heart for people. It is not natural; I was born selfish.

At the same time, I need others and cherish human relationships. I would never be a hermit. But to place interests of others before my own is something very difficult that requires the discipline of the Father. To learn to God-love others freely is something that comes with hard knocks. To God-love the Father in instant and total obedience requires training from above. Much must be learned. When the Apostle Paul wrote two mentoring letters to a young pastor named Timothy, he charged Timothy with many difficult things that have to do with loving God supremely though obedience and God-loving others as a pastor. He taught Timothy a very important lesson to remember.

> It is proper for the hard-toiling farmer to be the first to eat of the crop. Consider what I say; for the Lord will give you comprehension in all things. —2 Timothy 2:6–7

What reward is there when we are obedient to Jesus and His royal command to love God and others? It is the *obedient* who receive joy and peace in their soul in order to receive benefit and gain treasure in heaven. It is *we* who gain when we do unto others as we would have done to ourselves. The primary beneficiary of forgiveness is the one who forgives. Paul gave Timothy an important principle to think about when the going gets tough on the straight and narrow way of God-love. We are the first beneficiary when we walk the straight and narrow with God-love. Every step forward in God-love brings blessings in this life and reward in heaven.

> "Father, thank You for Your love toward me. Help me to comprehend that Your commands are for the good of all Your creation, but the greatest benefit comes to those who love and obey. Help me, Lord, to increase in love day by day, to walk the straight and narrow with the joy of knowing that great reward is being stored up for me in heaven. Amen."

Thursday: The Prodigal

Jesus' parable of the prodigal son is one that is precious to me and most other Christians (Luke 15:11–24). There was a Jewish father who had two sons under his *paideia*. The older son seemed to be compliant, but the younger son chafed under the discipline and decided to leave. He asked the father for the part of the inheritance that would fall to him and left home to gratify his supposed needs, following wherever his appetites led.

When his money was all spent on wine, prostitutes, and wild living, he found that he had no friends left. He hit the bottom of the barrel, a miserable Jewish lad feeding pigs and eating their leftovers. But Jesus said that in his misery the boy "came to himself." The boy thought, *I will go home because even the slaves eat better there. I will apologize to my father, seek his forgiveness, and ask him if I can be a slave in his house.* So he went on his way hungry, ragged, and barefoot, reciting over and over the speech he would give his angry dad. But something unexpected happened when he approached home.

> Even while he was far off, his father saw him and had compassion on him and embraced him with tears and kissed him. And the son said to him, "Father, I have sinned against heaven and before you. I no longer deserve to be your son. Make me one of your hired hands." But the father said to his slaves, "Quickly, bring out the best robe and put it on him and sandals for his feet. And bring the fattened calf and sacrifice it and eat it and let us be joyful! For this son of mine was dead and lives again, he had been lost but now he is found!" And they began to be merry. —Luke 15:20–24

The father did not even answer the speech of contrition that the son had prepared. The father sensed his son's genuine repentance, saw his miserable condition, and received his son back as a true son with joy and tears. God-love. With this parable, Jesus illustrated the love of Father God for those sinners who will sincerely repent and turn from their sins. When we sincerely receive those whom God has received as our brothers and sisters in Christ, even though we know of their past sins and weaknesses, we reflect God-love. Love as the Father loves.

> "Father God, help me to love like the father in the parable. Remind me that I came from the mire and the clay, and you had God-love for me. Amen."

Friday: The Homeboy

The father in the parable of the prodigal son actually had two prodigals. One son went away to spend his inheritance on wild living, and the other son stayed home; both became prodigals in different ways. I suppose I have experienced the problems of each of these young men. I came to repentance following a time of rebellion like the younger son and then lived with the Father for many years like the elder. The younger son refused the *paideia* of his father while the older homeboy did not learn from the father's example of God-love. The older son was obedient and compliant in the *paideia* but had not learned of mercy, grace, and God-love. Just about the time the homecoming party for the younger son got going strong, the older son came from the field, sweating and dirty with hard work. He asked a servant the cause of the noisy celebration and was told the father had received the younger brother back safe and sound.

> The older son was angry and did not want to come in. But his father came out pleading with him. But the son answered the father, "Look! I have served you for many years and never disobeyed your orders, and you never gave me even a young goat that I might be merry with my friends. But when this son of yours came, the one who ate up your living with prostitutes, you sacrifice a fattened calf." —Luke 15:28–30

Not many of us would have replied otherwise. It just does not seem right. But the older son made a statement that was not true. He claimed to have always obeyed his father, but he had just refused to have mercy on his younger brother just as his father had asked. If it were possible, we could perfectly obey the

Ten Commandments for our whole lives and yet be disobedient sinners if we do not have mercy on those to whom God shows mercy. People need to prove repentance by the fruit of repentance, but God-love gives them a chance. God-love receives as brothers and sisters those whom God has loved with salvation and a new birth.

> "Lord, You received me as a sinner and gave me a whole new life in Jesus Christ. You rescued me from darkness and brought me into the light. Keep me on the straight and narrow path of God-love. Teach me today so that I will reflect Your mercy and grace toward my brothers and sisters in Christ. Amen."

Saturday: Learning to Think Like the Father

Who has understood God? The Apostle Paul wrote, "Who knew the mind of the Lord, or who became His advisor?" (Romans 11:34). One of the hardest things to do is to present the gospel to a senior citizen who has never before thought much about salvation, to the person facing the near end of life who has never cared about Jesus, or to the prodigal who has never returned home to the Father. Their question is, "Can someone live for a lifetime any way they want and have all the sins that I have and at the end just ask God to forgive?" I always answer, "If you genuinely ask with faith in Jesus, God will forgive." But that does not seem right in the minds of people in those situations. Genuine repentance with faith is hard to find at the end. It is the only absolution I can offer to a dying sinner. I tell those pitiful folks that we do not think about such things in the way God thinks about them. Under the Father's *paideia* we learn, by His Word, to mirror His thinking.

> "Come now, and let us reason together," says the LORD, "Though your sins are as scarlet, they will be as white as snow; though they are red like crimson, they will be like wool." ... Seek the LORD while He may be found; call upon Him while He is near. Let the wicked forsake his way and the unrighteous man his thoughts; and let him return to the LORD, and He will have compassion on him, and to our God, for He will abundantly pardon. "For My thoughts are not your thoughts, nor are your ways My ways," declares the LORD. "For as the heavens are higher than the earth, so are My ways higher than your ways and My thoughts than your thoughts." —Isaiah 1:18; 55:6–9 NASB

126

This is how God-love is manifested to us by the Father. Jesus, in His teaching, always asked us to demonstrate the same kind of mercy, grace, and God-love toward others as God has shown to us. It is an important lesson we learn about walking the straight and narrow in the Father's *paideia* school. Sometimes it does not seem right that some people who have filled their life with sin can find salvation at the end. But that is the Father's way of grace and mercy to those who truly repent and believe the good news.

> "Father, help me see Your mercy and grace. Teach me Your ways both for myself and others. Send me, Lord, to someone who thinks they have no hope so that I may tell them of Your ways. Amen."

Week 9

Forgiveness

Sunday: When the Path Narrows

There is offense and there are offenses, forgiveness and forgiving. Sometimes the harm done is so egregious, the pain so enormous, and the wounds so enduring that forgiveness seems to be a bridge too far.

Recently there was an officer of the law on trial for murder for shooting a totally innocent man who was unarmed. The officer was off duty and returning home after her shift. The victim lived in the apartment directly above her. The officer got off on the wrong floor and mistakenly entered the man's apartment, who was sitting at the kitchen table eating ice cream. She thought he was an intruder in her apartment and shot him dead. The victim was a good, kind, and godly man, who served God as a Bible teacher.

The officer was convicted and given a ten-year prison sentence. At the sentencing, the brother of the victim took the stand and forgave the officer and told her that he did not want her to go to prison. He went the extra mile and hugged her, saying her life would be better if she would receive Christ and become a Christian.

After sentencing, the judge left the bench and gave the officer a Bible and embraced the woman with tears. When I remember the forgiving act of that godly brother I think of my brothers, my sister, my wife and children, and the others I love dearly in my family. I wonder about my ability to forgive a similar offence against my loved ones. The forgiving brother walked the narrow path when it became narrow indeed.

> Let all bitter wickedness and anger and rage and shouting and slander be taken away from you, along with all evil. And be kind to one another, full of compassion, forgiving each other, as also God in Christ forgave you. —Ephesians 4:31–32

Unforgiveness leads us into bitterness, anger, rage, and many kinds of evil that make us enemies of our own soul. Forgiveness leads to godliness, joy, and peace of mind. And the testimony of Jesus Christ is preached to the world through His brothers and sisters who forgive and exhibit His forgiving spirit. There is no better way to understand the forgiveness of God than to receive it from the children of God. Seek forgiveness from God, and pass it along today for your eternal benefit and for the kingdom of God.

> "Father in heaven, take away all the bitterness, anger, rage, and every evil that may be hidden in my heart. Put God-love in the place of those things. Mold me into a person like Jesus who forgave my every offence against Him. Amen."

Monday: FOD

When I drove a truck into the aircraft factory, I always had to drive over a special grid-type plate that removed any pebbles or other objects that may have been stuck in the tire tread. Then I had to get out of the truck and inspect the tires for anything that may have been missed. An employee would check to see that there was no FOD (foreign object debris) my truck might leave on the pavement. A sweeper truck was kept in constant operation to ensure that the pavement and tarmac was absolutely clean. These measures were in place because even a small rock could have been sucked up into a powerful jet engine and caused severe damage to the turbine.

There are items of unforgiveness in my heart that are like FOD that have to be continually cleaned up with diligence. I am thinking of one particular incident that happened many years ago, a humiliation that wounded me severely. I have forgiven the person, but the person has been a personality in the media, and every time I see that person the old angst arises, and my ears burn with resentment. In the scheme of my whole life the offense was a little thing that can cause damage to my soul far beyond the significance of that offence. I have to keep forgiving and praying for the person.

> Then Peter came to Him and said, "Lord, how often when my brother sins against me should I forgive him? As many as seven times?" Jesus said to him, "I say to you not up to seven times, but as many as seventy times seven." —Matthew 18:21–22

We do not know if Peter was talking about seven different offences or the same sin committed seven times. The remembrance of wrongdoing can certainly come to our minds 490 times. He did not say whether the sin of his brother was great or small. The point is that unforgiveness is incompatible with God-love. God forgives and forgets our sins. But as humans we cannot forget some things. We have to repeat the process of forgiveness over and over to protect that which God has given us. And who can say that God does not have to continually forgive us for our failures great and small?

> "Father, be merciful to me. Help me to have mercy on others and forgive as You have forgiven me many times. Help me deal with memories of wrong that I cannot shake but can continually forgive. Amen."

Tuesday: Boundaries

Sometimes it is necessary to forgive some people from our heart but in God-love separate ourselves from them. I do not think it is biblical to continually expose myself to toxic people, dangerous circumstances, or poisonous relationships. Joseph forgave his brothers yet tested them before he revealed his identity (Genesis 43-45). Jesus avoided King Herod Antipas who wanted to kill Him before the Lord could reach the goal of the Cross (Luke 13:31–33). Barnabas, the Son of Compassion, ended his partnership with the Apostle Paul and went his separate way (Acts 15:36–39).

Each of these were prime examples of compassionate and forgiving people who faithfully walked the straight and narrow way of God-love, never returning evil for evil, but who also drew boundaries around their lives to protect themselves. Only when Joseph saw that his brothers spoke truthfully and became convinced of the repentance of his brothers and their true change of heart did he make himself vulnerable to them. It is a long and complicated story that you can read about in Genesis. Joseph's goal was realized when the older brother, who had acted so cruelly and violently against him, offered to sacrifice himself in God-love for the sake of his younger brother and his father. What a wonderful reconciliation Joseph made with them then.

> Then Joseph said to his brothers, "I am Joseph! Is my father still alive?" But his brothers could not answer him, for they were dismayed at his presence. Then Joseph said to his brothers, "Please come closer to me." And they came closer. And he said, "I am your brother Joseph, whom you sold into Egypt. Now do not be grieved or angry with yourselves, because you sold me here, for God sent me before you to preserve life." —Genesis 45:3–5 NASB

Apart from the life of Christ, there is no better example of how to walk the straight and narrow path of God-love than that of Joseph, son of Jacob, called Zaphenath-Paneah ("the one who furnishes the nourishment of life"), and the prime minister to Pharaoh, king of Egypt. Being in perfect position to take vengeance on those who harmed him, Joseph never returned evil for evil. His zeal became the saving of lives. Neither did he allow his brothers, or anyone else, to be in a position to harm him again. *God-love.*

> "Father God, make me into a person like Joseph. Give me, please, the wisdom You gave him in relationships with others. Be with me as You were with Joseph that I may always act with God-love. Amen."

Wednesday: Freedom

I am a born sinner, "inclined to all evil, and that continually," as the catechism states. But I am now a redeemed man who has been saved by grace and forgiven by God. I know what it is like to be a slave of sin, and I know what it is like to be free. It is better to be free. I have been ravaged by repressed anger, torn asunder by silent rage, and subject to every whim of my body. The love of God has freed me from those things, and I rejoice each day in my freedom.

One of the tools that has been furnished to me to break the chains of anger is to offer free and sincere forgiveness to others from my heart. As much as God has enabled me to do this, so much has freedom been realized in my life. It is rarely possible to tell those whom I have forgiven because that seems to insult them and only inflames the situation, and perhaps I am wrong. Sometimes I imagine an offense when there is none. People seldom ask for forgiveness, so a silent attitude of forgiveness is for my sake to keep me at peace. I have found the best way to do this is to pray for those who may have offended me and intercede with God to forgive them for anything, real or imagined, that they may have done against me. Jesus is our example, and the offenses against Him were real.

> When they came upon the place called "The Skull," they crucified Him and the criminals, one on the right and one on the left. But Jesus kept saying, "Father, forgive them, for they do not know what they are doing." —Luke 23:33–34

Who were "they" for whom Jesus interceded? The ones who nailed His hands, the ones who divided His garments, the ones who conspired against Him, the ones who falsely accused Him, the feckless governor who condemned Him, the soldiers who beat and scourged Him, the ones who reviled Him at Golgotha, and the ones who did not care at all. Real freedom and true peace of mind come through free forgiveness from the heart. It will help us stay on the straight and narrow.

> Father, I am thinking of one for whom I have anger. I pray, Lord, that You hold nothing against them for what harm they have done to me. Teach me, Father, the way of free forgiveness that I may be free. In Jesus' name I pray. Amen."

Thursday: Justice and Forgiveness

It is a difficult thing to balance justice and forgiveness. Debbie Morris had to do just that when she was only sixteen years of age. On a warm summer evening in Madisonville, Louisiana, she was assaulted and kidnapped by Robert Willie and Joseph Vaccaro as she and her boyfriend sat in a car eating ice cream. Her boyfriend was tied to a tree, tortured, and left for dead. He survived but was permanently disabled. Eight days earlier, Willie and Joseph had raped and murdered a woman and threw her body into a pit. After taking Debbie, they continually threatened to kill her, and they raped her numerous times before letting her go on a country road. Debbie's testimony put Willie in the electric chair. I can only imagine the struggle that she had in balancing justice and forgiveness. She could only find forgiveness in her heart for them by giving it up totally to God. She said it was a process that extended out for years, and she wrote about it in *Forgiving the Dead Man Walking*, a book I highly recommend. She came to understand that she had to forgive Willie to obtain her own peace, but at the same time was obligated to tell the truth and let the justice system take its course. She interceded with God for Willie but had no authority to show mercy in the criminal justice system.

> The exercise of justice is joy for the righteous, but is terror to the workers of iniquity. —Proverbs 21:15 NASB

We cannot forgive the sins of others; only God can do that. We cannot forgive crimes, only judges and governors have that authority. We can only forgive criminals for what harm they may have done to us and plead with God to have mercy on them in judgment. Misplaced mercy on the wicked can pervert justice for the weak and deny justice to the oppressed. God has given us human authorities to carry out punishment on earth. Seek justice, but leave retribution to judges and juries and eternal judgment to God. God is much better than we at balancing justice, mercy, and forgiveness. Let Him be the judge of it and forgive from the heart.

> "Lord God, You are perfectly just, extending mercy and forgiveness in perfect proportion. I cannot have Your perfect wisdom and love. Yet I ask You for the God-love that is guided by wisdom. Help me to seek justice for others, for the poor and oppressed as well as the wicked. Help me to be a forgiving, merciful, and just person. In Jesus' name. Amen."

Friday: The Stone Wall

There is a stone wall facing me laid across the straight and narrow path of God-love: my unforgiveness. I know that I should, I must, forgive according to the Word of God, but sometimes there is resistance in me that is difficult to deal with. This is especially true when someone who has continually hurt me does not *ever* ask for forgiveness. It is difficult to forgive when it does not seem to make sense. Sometimes the offenses are small and insignificant except that they occur over and over again and I cannot escape them. To remain on the straight and narrow, I have to stay in a constant state of forgiveness. In prayer, I ask the Lord to help me, and I always get the same answer, "I have forgiven *you* many times."

Jesus told a parable about a king who had a servant who owed a debt that was impossible to repay. The man pleaded with the king saying, "Lord, have patience, I will pay you all." The king had compassion upon the man and forgave his debt. That man was owed a much smaller debt by another servant, a tiny fraction of what the first servant had owed. The second servant pleaded, "Have patience, I will pay you all." The first servant refused to forgive and threw the second servant into prison and sold his wife and children into slavery.

> Then his lord called the first servant and said to him, "Wicked servant! I forgave all that debt because you begged me. Was it not also right for you to have compassion for your fellow servant as I also had compassion on you?" And his lord was very angry and gave him over to the torturers until he repaid everything he owed. This also will My heavenly Father do for each one of you, unless you forgive your brother from the heart. —Matthew 18:32–35

Gulp. Not much can be said to add or detract from what Jesus said. He explained himself very well. We can only go forward on the straight and narrow for it is a one-way path, dissolving behind us into yesterday. For our own benefit, we must find some way to get over the stone wall of unforgiveness *today*.

> "Lord, help me over that stone wall of unforgiveness today. Better yet, Lord, help me to tear down the wall with God-love and forgiveness. Help me to just let go of resentment and bitterness that I may walk with sweet freedom down the straight and narrow. Amen."

Saturday: Letting Go

Some of the most heartfelt prayers I have ever written are in the margins of my first-year Greek grammar book. It was a real struggle for me. There were nouns and verbs and participles in a foreign alphabet with some really weird characters. I failed the first year. I took it again with a better outcome, and the advanced level went considerably better. It was an ordeal in those days.

But when I found my mature faith, I fell in love with the original language of the New Testament. Word study helps me better understand what God, through the writers of the Bible, is trying to say to me. The study of the word *agape* (God-love) and its nuances and uses in the New Testament led to this devotional. There is another word that has impacted me as I have written this chapter. It is the word that is translated "I forgive": *aphiémi.* It literally means to "let go." This is what Jesus said about "letting go" of offenses and forgiving from the heart:

> For if you forgive (*aphiémi*) people their wrongdoing, your Father in heaven will also forgive you. But if you do not forgive people, neither will your Father forgive your wrongdoing. —Matthew 6:14–15

The Father in heaven will let go of His anger at our sins if we will let go of our anger against others who have sinned against us. He will let go of and remit our sins if we forgive others. But if we do not let go of anger and let the offence remain, neither will the Father let go of His anger at our sins. He will hold on to them.

I remember the best advice that I ever received from a Christian friend who counseled me when I was having conflict with another friend: "George, *just let it go.*" I do not know why we want to hold on to anger and resentment when we could be released from their corrosive effects by forgiveness. It is the surest way to find favor with Almighty God, to find peace in our heart and, perhaps, repair or find a relationship with another.

> "Father in heaven, forgive me please where I have been unforgiving. I will forgive others. So I plead for grace that I may show the mercy and forgiveness You have shown me. Shine Your light upon the dark places of my soul to find the darkness of anger, resentment, and unforgiveness. Lead me out of the darkness into the light of God-love. Amen."

Week 10

The Shepherd

Sunday: The One Who Loves

I am not alone on the straight and narrow. There is a Shepherd with me whose God-love is so great He pledged His life and soul to keep me on the straight and narrow path and will do everything in His power to see that I make it all the way home. He is the Good Shepherd, Jesus Christ my Lord.

The shepherd-sheep metaphor is found throughout the Bible. God calls Himself the Shepherd of Israel and wants the leaders of the nation to be like shepherds. When Jacob blessed Joseph, he called the Lord, "The God who has been my shepherd all my life to this day" (Genesis 48:15 NASB). When the people are ill led, God says they are like sheep without a shepherd. He gave me a Good Shepherd in Jesus. I am well led down the path, and He is One who leads me with everlasting God-love. When I wander off the path, He brings me back. When I am afraid, He comforts me. He knows me, and I know Him.

> I am the Good Shepherd. The Good Shepherd lays down His life for the sheep ... I am the Good Shepherd and I know My sheep and My sheep know me ... the Father knows Me, and I know the Father, so I lay down My life for the sheep. —John 10:11, 14–15

Sometimes we think we are alone on the path, especially when it seems that God-love is not returned from others, we just do not feel like we are making progress, or we do not sense the closeness of Jesus. Think of the God-love of Jesus. He did not put on flesh to walk up Calvary while suffering indignity, incredible torture, and devastation of soul just to abandon us on the way. In love, He did it to save us and to keep us on the straight and narrow path of God-love. If we seem to be off the path and do not know the way back, we need to go to prayer with the Bible, listening for the voice of the Good Shepherd.

> "Jesus, Your presence with me is my hope. Even though the road is straight, I stupidly lose my way. I will listen for Your voice, for You constantly speak to my soul. So I will not fear any danger, and I cannot wander if I stay close as You lead me down the straight and narrow. Amen."

Monday: The Shepherd Leader

The best leaders I have ever known have been shepherd leaders. They are the ones who have God-love and are concerned about the people they lead. I have seen many leaders who gave fine speeches and had well-thought-out agendas and a good understanding of administration who did not excel and often failed because they were not good shepherds. They had little love for the sheep and expended all their efforts on climbing the ladder of success. When the opportunities came, they used people to further their own goals. When hard times came, they ran away to find another flock to serve them. The good leaders are vitally concerned with the welfare of the people they lead. As much as they are able, they protect the sheep from harm. They measure their success by the success of the flock, trusting the Good Shepherd to take care of them. And they *never* run away from trouble.

> I am the Good Shepherd. The Good Shepherd lays down His life for the sheep. The hired hand, not being a shepherd who owns the sheep, realizes the wolf is coming and deserts the sheep and runs away, and the wolf seizes them and scatters them. —John 10:11–12

Almost all of us are leaders in one way or another. Christians have responsibilities as leaders in the church, government, business, society, and in their families. Whether it is guiding a nation, an institution, a business, or a child, the best leaders are shepherd leaders. When we follow Jesus' commands to love God supremely and God-love others sincerely, the success of the ones we lead becomes our success and their problems become our business. We share their joy and empathize with their pain. When we follow Jesus' example and encourage others to find the narrow path of God-love and convince others to return to the path, we know that we are leaders imitating the Good Shepherd.

> "Lord, You have been so good to me. You have called to me and cared for me as I have tried to follow You down the straight and narrow way. When I have strayed, You came for me. When I stumbled, You lifted me up. Help me to be that kind of a shepherd to others, not in an intrusive or annoying way, but in a merciful way. I want to be a good shepherd like You. Amen."

Tuesday: The Flock

I travel with the flock down the narrow path of God-love. There are no go-it-alone sheep in the fold of Christ, for He founded a community of faith. Around the fifth century there came about a peculiar group of ascetics called stylites. They were hermits who sat upon tall pillars to separate themselves from the temptations of the world. The inspiration for these fellows was Simeon Stylites the Elder who parked himself on a pillar and stayed there without coming down for thirty-seven years. In that lonely, contemplative perch, it seemed easy to walk the narrow path. There were no human relationships to worry about, no other sheep to annoy Simeon, no conflicts, no worrisome family problems, and most of all, the world and all its ways were far from stylites. People considered him to be a most holy man and served him by passing up food and taking care of the waste he sent down—I hope they used different buckets. Lightning, among other things, was a grave hazard that helped bring the practice to an end. But I think the real end of it came for the same reason almost all solitary asceticism ended: the utter futility and waste of a life devoid of human relationships. The prophecy of Jesus Christ is that He will come to be our shepherd, and we will be His flock.

> Behold, the Lord GOD will come with might, with His arm ruling for Him. Behold, His reward is with Him and His recompense before Him. Like a shepherd He will tend His flock, in His arm He will gather the lambs and carry them in His bosom; He will gently lead the nursing ewes. —Isaiah 40:10–11 NASB

We travel with the flock down a path that leads straight through this world with dangers on the right and the left. We need the church and the church needs us because we are opposed all the way by a culture that does not love God. While on the path of God-love we are not *of* the world but are making our way *through* the world to a fold in heaven along with many other sheep. We have the Good Shepherd out front to lead us, tend to our needs, protect us from the evil one, and carry the weak in the bosom of His grace.

> "Jesus, I know You are the Good Shepherd. I cannot travel this path of God-love without You. Help me, Lord, when I act stupidly or have trouble with the other sheep. Thank You for the flock I travel with. Help me to be a loving part of it. Amen."

Wednesday: The Shepherd-Sheep

Have you ever known someone who was like a protective, kind, and generous shepherd but refused to let anyone do something good for them? If you try to help them freely, they insist on paying, not wanting to be under some obligation. Or if you want to give them a gift, they refuse in the spirit of, "It is better to give than to receive." They deny every compliment, deflect even well-deserved praise, and take every action not to appear vainglorious. They showed God-love to others but would not receive the least shepherding. They forgot that all of Christ's sheep are called to be shepherds as well—shepherd-sheep.

When I used to go visit my mother, I would drive by a small flock of sheep near her home that was tended by three llamas. In the middle of the pasture there was a mound of earth where one llama would stand, as though on guard, and watch everything that was going on. The llamas would take turns on guard duty. The farmer was a shepherd to the llamas, and the llamas were a shepherd to him by guarding his sheep and looking out for his interests. They *all* received love from one another. In Jesus' flock, the ones He has appointed shepherds to oversee his people are sheep too. Together we walk the straight and narrow.

> Pay attention to yourselves and to all the flock, in which the Holy Spirit has appointed you overseers to shepherd the church of God, which he bought with His own blood. —Acts 20:28

It is a great blessing to be a shepherd, to be a pastor and to *act* with God-love toward others. Why should the shepherd deny similar blessings to the sheep? If we are "laity" and have not received an ordination in an institution of men, we should still consider ourselves to be shepherds. In this arrangement, believers look

152

out for other believers. The sheep are shepherds to each other and look after the appointed shepherd also. May we do good to others in God-love and graciously receive the same.

> "Father in heaven, make me a shepherd for Your people, my brothers and sisters in Christ. Help me to be a blessing and a help to all of them. And give me grace that I may receive God-love from them, and together we will be blessed above all the people of the earth. In Jesus' name, amen."

Thursday: The Other Sheep

When I was a kid, I loved Superman. Anytime I had a quarter I would go to the drugstore and buy a Superman comic book, a Coke, and a piece of bubblegum for a delightful afternoon. I especially liked his superpower of X-ray vision where he could see through walls of concrete and steel. Sometimes comic books would have advertisements for X-ray glasses. The ad claimed you could see through clothing and illustrated it with a goofy cartoon character. I never ordered one, so I do not know if it worked, but it was a mighty temptation for a thirteen-year-old boy.

The ability to see beyond natural eyesight and to observe things, even though line of sight is blocked, is a driving force of technology for civilian and military use. Remote cameras are in use everywhere. They help us secure our homes and businesses, spy out the enemy, and view the hidden side of the moon and the surface of Mars. As a pastor, I have often wished that the people could have X-ray glasses to look through the walls of the church to see the people outside who need Jesus the Good Shepherd. Jesus said there are "other sheep" outside of the fold that need to be brought in.

> Just as the Father knows Me, I also know the Father, and I lay down My life for the sheep. I have other sheep that are not of this fold. It is necessary for Me to bring them in, and they will become My sheep with one shepherd. —John 10:15–16

The disciples who first received these words of Jesus had no way of seeing the billions of people who now claim Jesus as their Good Shepherd. But Jesus always sees the "other sheep," and we should look for them also. The Bible says Jesus viewed the people with great compassion because they were like "sheep without a shepherd". (Matthew 9:36; Mark 6:34) I think the reason we do not feel compassion toward those who are not with us on the straight and narrow way is that we simply do not see the "other sheep." We should look for them with compassion and invite them to travel the straight and narrow way of God-love. Tell them about the Good Shepherd who has been so good to us.

> "Jesus, help me to see the other sheep with compassion and God-love. Put words in my mouth to express how good You have been to me and what a wonderful thing it is to have a Good Shepherd. Amen."

Friday: The Shepherd's Rod

There is no passage of the Bible heard more often at the funeral of a believer than Psalm 23. But to my way of thinking, the psalm is more for everyday living than a text for a funeral message. King David, a shepherd himself, wrote the psalm. I agree with him; the Lord is *my* Shepherd. Without Him I could never even *find* the straight and narrow way of God-love, much less stay on it. I feel no lack of anything with Him. He makes me rest when I am weary, soothes my mind when I am agitated, and leads me down the "path of righteousness" with God-love for Him and for the flock. The psalm reads, "Your rod and Your staff, they comfort me" (v. 4 NASB). It teaches me something about how to be a pastor, a shepherd in the mold of the Great Shepherd. It tells me that I not only must do my best to care for the sheep but also I must do my best to protect the flock from the wolf that wishes to scatter the flock and the thief who comes to kill and destroy. The final three verses of the psalm speak to us of the shepherd-warrior who defends the sheep.

> Even though I walk through the valley of the shadow of death, I fear no evil, for You are with me; Your rod and Your staff, they comfort me. You prepare a table before me in the presence of my enemies; You have anointed my head with oil; my cup overflows. Surely goodness and lovingkindness will follow me all the days of my life, and I will dwell in the house of the LORD forever." —Psalm 23:4–6 NASB

The rod of the shepherd was a deadly weapon. It was a stout club with which the shepherd bludgeoned the enemies of the flock. David, a shepherd himself, knew the use of the rod as a weapon to defend himself and the sheep. David told King Saul that when a lion tried to take a lamb from his flock, he killed the lion by grabbing its beard and striking it (1 Samuel 17:34–35). David realized the worth of a weapon to do good for others. Nature itself teaches us that we should defend our family and the flock with the fierceness of a mama bear defending her cubs. There is no God-love or virtue in allowing violent people to kill us or our families, but there is God-love in being a shepherd with a sturdy rod who knows how to protect the sheep.

> "Dear Lord, give me the courage and strength to defend myself and the flock from violent men. Thank You for the means to protect the innocent from the evil and the violent. Increase my God-love that I may always act with righteous motives and a pure heart. In Jesus' name, amen."

Saturday: The Sheep Dog

One thing I learned while serving as chaplain for law enforcement is that while the sheep love the shepherd, they hate the sheepdog. When the officers responded to a difficult domestic situation, I tried to gather the family to pray for familial peace—if they would receive it. I occupied them while the officers separated the combatants to lay down the law. I have prayed with atheists, Jews, Christians, Muslims, Hindus, and the clueless. If I just prayed to Almighty God for love to reign, no one seemed to be offended. Everyone loves the shepherd.

The officers do not fare so well with the goodwill of the combatants. They are just trying to keep two (or more) people from fighting with, or possibly killing, each other. The officers may receive the vilest of insults and verbal abuse, but they follow their training and respond with measured firmness. Of course, there are exceptions to this both among officers and chaplains, but for the most part, both the acts of the officers and the acts of the chaplain are acts of love. But the sheep do not think the sheepdog loves them at all.

> Let every soul be subject to governing authorities. For there is no authority except by God, and the ones that exist are appointed by God. ... For the rulers are not a terror to those who do good but to those who do evil. Do you want no fear of the authorities? Do good, and you will have praise from the same; for he is a servant of God to you for good. —Romans 13:1, 3–4a
>
> Submit to every government of men for the sake of the Lord, whether to a king as being in authority, or governors sent by him to punish evildoers and

to praise those who do good. Because by the will of God they are doing good to muzzle the ignorance of senseless men. —1 Peter 2:13–15

New officers come into service being very idealistic, wanting to live up to the motto, "Protect and Serve." They are the young sheepdogs yearning to get between the sheep and the wolf to save the flock. But often they have the spirit beaten out of them by the sheep they are trying to protect. Law enforcement officers are a good opportunity for Jesus' sheep to show some God-love with respect, encouragement, and appreciation for their service as sheepdogs.

"Lord, thank You for the ones who get between me and the wolf. They do not run away from gunfire but run toward it. Protect them, Lord, and help me to be respectful and compliant. Amen."

Week 11

Joy

Sunday: Joyless Religion

I can think of nothing so dispiriting as joyless religion. Going through the motions of piety and jumping through hoops for the sake of rule keeping does not bring joy. I believe in being reverent and obedient to Jesus' commands, but without joy it becomes drudgery. God-love brings joy on the straight and narrow way. I have the prospect of heaven and walk with the peace of God residing in my soul! It seems to me that things are right, that what I do pleases God, for the most part, and the Holy Spirit reassures and gives me strength. Jesus seems to walk closely, step-by-step. The love of God and my God-love for Him propels me down the path with joy. There is no senseless toil ahead of me, only gladness and delight in the Lord and the life He has given me.

> I have set the LORD continually before me; because He is at my right hand, I will not be shaken. Therefore, my heart is glad and my glory rejoices; my flesh also will dwell securely. For You will not abandon my soul to Sheol [the abode of the dead]; nor will You allow Your Holy One to undergo decay. You will make known to me the path of life; in Your presence is fullness of joy; in Your right hand there are pleasures forever. — Psalm 16:8–11 NASB

There is always meaningful work ahead of us on the straight and narrow. Difficulties may abound and monsters stalk the way, but because of God-love we press forward with joy. We know God loves us, and we will reach our goal and have the object of our desire. Victory is ours, and a crown awaits us in heaven. So, give a shout of "Hallelujah!" for another day on the path of God-love.

"Father in heaven, thank You for the life You have given me. Thank You for the joy Your love brings forth in me. I love You, God; I will show my love by my obedience. You have given me peace of soul and the hope of pleasures at Your right hand forevermore—such joy! You give me the desires of my heart. Amen."

Monday: "Eureka!"

The exclamation, "Eureka!" is attributed to Archimedes of ancient Greece. It means, "I have found it!" Supposedly, he was sitting in a bath when he thought of the solution to the difficult problem of testing gold for purity. He shouted, "Eureka! I have found it," as he ran naked out of the bath. Others have experienced eureka moments of discovery. Newton experienced it when he discovered gravity, Einstein when theorizing about relativity. Poe wrote a poem about it, and prospectors for gold helped make it the state motto of California. It is an exclamation of great joy at the moment of discovery or the instant of finding something that was lost.

I had a eureka moment when I found that God-love is the key to every aspect of following the straight and narrow way of Christ. It unlocked the shackles of legalism and liberated me to live in the grace of God. God's love for me and my love for Him and others broke my addictions. I discovered, by the Holy Spirit, the power to live by the royal law of the Lord; to love God supremely and God-love others sincerely. It became the solution to every problem of relationship in my life. *Eureka!* I found it.

> And He [Jesus] told them this parable, "What man of you having one hundred sheep having lost one of them does not leave the ninety-nine in the desert and look for the lost one until he finds it? And having found it, he puts it on his shoulders rejoicing. When he comes to the house, he calls together friends and neighbors and says to them, 'Rejoice with me because I have found my lost sheep!' I say to you that there is more joy in heaven over one sinner who repents than over ninety-nine righteous who have no need of repentance." —Luke 15:3–7

Heaven also seems to have its eureka moments of joy. God loves us so much that He provided His own Son that whoever has faith in Him would "not perish but have eternal life." They would not remain lost but be found. His faithful ones would walk the straight and narrow with God-love for Him. God experiences joy because He is delighted that we have been found and the voice of Christ resounds in heaven, "Joy! I have found My lost sheep!"

> "Father God, I am filled with joy because You found me. Everything is going to turn out well because You love me. There is joy in Your presence forevermore. Amen."

Tuesday: I Will Win

In 1990, in promoting the upcoming World Cup soccer tournament in Italy, the BBC began promoting their broadcast with the soundtrack of an Italian operatic aria, "Nessun Dorma" from *Turandot* by Puccini. It was sung by the incomparable tenor Luciano Pavarotti and became an instant hit with highbrow fans and soccer hooligans alike. The opera is about a man in China who wants to marry a reluctant princess. They make a deal that if she can guess his name by dawn he will die, but if not, they will marry. (Hey! It's *opera*, okay?) Nessun Dorma means, "Let no one sleep." I wouldn't. As dawn approaches the man realizes he is going to win, and he joyfully concludes the aria, "All'alba vincerò! Vincerò! Vincerò!" "At dawn, I will win! I will win! I will win!" Pavarotti makes it one of the most moving arias I have ever heard.

But I have a greater joy than I could ever find from winning a game by kicking a ball into a net. It is in winning over the temptations and trials that could take me off the straight and narrow path in defeat. I rejoice in knowing that the God-who-loves-me has equipped me to face every battle on the narrow way. Sometimes it seems that the night of trial will never end. But I see a light on the horizon that tells me dawn is approaching, and I am confident that with the grace of Christ and His love I will conquer all. I will win! I will win! I will win!

> Who will separate us from the God-love of Christ? Will pressure, or distress, or persecution, or hunger, or nakedness, or danger, or sword? Just as it is written, "For Your sake we are being put to death; all day long we are considered as sheep for slaughter." But in all this we are overwhelming victors through the One who God-loves us. —Romans 8:35–37

There is great joy when we understand that through the God-love of Christ we will win! There is no requirement of obedience on the straight and narrow that cannot be fulfilled by loving God supremely and God-loving others sincerely. There is no battle that cannot be won in Jesus' name.

> "My Lord, You give me the victory in Jesus Christ! What joy You give to me. I will not doubt Your love or Your grace. Purify my heart and fill me with Your Spirit that I may love and win! Amen."

Wednesday: Sacrifice

We have no greater respect than for the ones who risk life and limb for us. The events of 9/11 taught us that there are brave men and women who are anxious to give their "full measure of devotion" because of their love for their fellow citizens. My father and my father-in-law both sacrificed four years of the prime of their youth to fight against tyranny and evil in World War II—one in the European theater and the other in the Pacific. The smell of the dead buried in the rubble of towns and villages of Europe lingers in the minds of veterans. The terror of Guadalcanal remains with their memory and takes them back to the trench where fear gripped them as they hid as best they could from the blast of bombs. They were there because of war; they swallowed fear and fought because of their love for the ones back home and their comrades in arms. Both of them said something with different words but the same meaning. "War is more horrible than you can imagine. I would never want to do it again. But I am glad I was there because it made me into the man that I am." Both of the men had joy because of their sacrifice, although they never said they were happy when they were at war.

> Let us lay aside every impediment and besetting sin and let us run with endurance the race that is laid out before us. Focus on Jesus, the founder and perfecter of our faith, who for the joy set before Him endured the cross, despising the shame, and sat down at the right hand of the throne of God. —Hebrews 12:1–2

Jesus made a sacrifice on Mount Calvary because He loves the Father supremely and God-loves us sincerely. He found joy in the agony because He realized the greatness of the things He was doing for us. There are sacrifices that must be made to remain on the straight and narrow. Jesus said that if we wish to come after Him, we must deny ourselves to take up our cross and follow Him. We must imitate His sacrifice, in a spiritual manner, becoming a living sacrifice to God. If we do, we will find joy in a sacrificial way of living and walking like Jesus on the straight and narrow.

> "Dear Lord, please receive me as a living sacrifice to You. Help me as I try to deny myself as Jesus commanded. Show me the way of God-love so that I may have joy as I travel the narrow way. Amen."

Thursday: Sing for Joy

Real men sing really loud in church. That is the philosophy I brought home from a men's conference where I sang with thirty thousand other guys who could not sing any better than I. Some were better than others, but *everyone* was loud. It seemed as though God was very near as we lifted the roof of that enclosed stadium in praise and love for Jesus. I like to get some spiritual song wedged in my head and sing throughout the day. But sometimes a secular tune intrudes and gets stuck there. There is nothing wrong with that, but I really love to sing about Jesus and the God-love we share. So, I do my best to get the world's tunes replaced by heavenly ones.

That is one of the reasons I go to church regularly. I love to sing hands-in-the-air praises to the one who is worthy because with His blood He purchased my soul unto God. The songs stick with me for days. I feel strengthened and encouraged when I sing for joy about the One who God-loves and accompanies me as I walk down the narrow path. When I look at that great worship service in heaven described in Revelation 4 and 5, I try to imagine the volume of noise and the joy of those billions of beings from heaven and earth who praise and sing around the throne of God. They even sing *new* songs.

> And they sang a new song, "Worthy are You [Jesus], to take up the scroll and open the seals because You were slain and with your blood you purchased unto God people from every race and language and nation and made them for our God a kingdom and priests, and they will rule on the earth." —Revelation 5:9–10

170

When we think about what Jesus has done for us, it is easier to sing for joy as we go along the path. By His blood He saved us and transformed our lives. That is what God-love accomplished for us. By our love for Him and our God-love toward others we stay on the straight and narrow, but without Jesus we could never even find the way.

> "You are worthy, Lord Jesus, to receive honor and glory and blessing. For You saved my soul along with countless other human souls. I love You, Lord, I worship You, and I adore You. Thank You for Your grace and mercy. May I live likewise. Amen."

Friday: Joy of a Father

I can only remember a few times when my father wept. He was one of those WWII guys who just sucked it up and moved on. The time I can remember that brought him to tears was when I brought a report card home from school with all Fs—even in gym class. It wasn't that I did not learn, but I preferred to go with Horatio Hornblower on the high seas, to be taken by C. S. Forrester into battle with wooden ships and iron men, to be taken by Jack London into adventure with White Fang in the frozen north, to seek perfect revenge with the Count of Monte Cristo, and any other adventure I could find at the library. Tests were a bore I enlivened by making sequential patterns out of multiple-choice boxes.

My noncompliant behavior was atrocious. I will never forget the defeated look on my father's face when he read that report card and the comments of the teachers. I eventually saw the benefit in being educated, but it took years to realize the one thing my father really wanted for me—to grow up to be a godly man. When he was an old man and I was middle-aged, my father got to see me deliver a Sunday morning sermon in church. I will never forget the joy I saw in my father's face as I watched him from the pulpit. The Bible speaks of a time when God's wayward children will be restored to a right relationship with Him.

> The LORD your God is in your midst, a victorious warrior. He will exult over you with joy, He will be quiet in His love, He will rejoice over you with shouts of joy. —Zephaniah 3:17 NASB

Just as we rejoice over the success of our children, our Heavenly Father also has joy when we are in right relationship with Him through grace and the God-love that brings obedience. God is pleased with us when we love Him with all our heart, soul, mind, and strength and others as ourselves. He is delighted when we prove our love by the way we walk the straight and narrow path.

> "God I am not worthy to be called Your son. I have sinned against You and harmed others. But You have restored my soul and set my feet upon the rock, which is Christ Jesus. You have given me success on the narrow way. May You have great joy in Your adopted son, a sinner transformed by Your grace. Amen."

Saturday: Persecution

It is only God-love that finds joy in persecution. Perhaps joy is in it because we have a certain assurance that we are in right relationship with God and are holding on to eternal life no matter what people do to us. The Bible says that in the last days the saints will be overcome by Satan, but they will be victorious "by the blood of the lamb and the word of their testimony, and they did not love their lives even unto death" (Revelation 12:11). There is joy in being faithful to our testimony against all odds. Because of our love for Jesus and for the God-love of our own souls, we hold fast to eternal life. But the world does not think the way we do. It is hard for us to understand their fury and their desire to harm us just because of what we believe. Sometimes believers suffer horribly in this world. But for most of us, it is just words that are hurled at us. Jesus said any persecution for His name's sake is an occasion for joy.

> Blessed-happy are you when men detest you and when they cast you out and they reproach you and throw out your name as evil because of the Son of Man. Rejoice in that day and leap for joy, for look, your reward is great in heaven. —Luke 6:22–23

It is because of this kind of persecution that most believers stay out of sight and silent about their faith. We need to tell people about our love of Jesus. That does not mean we preach sermons or condemn others. It means that the people acquainted with us know we are Christian. It means that our lives bring forth the deeds of God-love that are a testimony for Christ that cannot be denied. By our actions and graceful acknowledgement of Jesus Christ, we will always cast the seed of the gospel, and our reward will be great in heaven because we are fruitful. Who cares if some people detest us? The Eternal One loves us. What if we suffer reproach for the name of Jesus? There is the Lord who will say at the last, "Well done, good and faithful servant. You were faithful over a few things, I will appoint you over many things. Enter into the joy of your Lord" (Matthew 25:23).

> "Dear Lord, more than anything, I want to hear from You that I have been faithful over a few things. I love You more than the praise of men, and Your rebuke is more valuable to me than the kisses of this world. I want to enter into Your joy. Amen."

Week 12

Oneness

Sunday: The Prayer for Me

On the night he was betrayed, Jesus taught His disciples many things as they walked to the Mount of Olives from the upper room where they had shared the Last Supper. Later that evening, before His agony in Gethsemane, Jesus prayed for the disciples and included in that prayer a supplication for me and for all those who would believe because of the testimony of those eleven remaining disciples. I do not know when I personalized this prayer and understood that I could be one with God. But I read it many times before it struck me that I could enter into that kind of intimate relationship with the Almighty.

> For them I sanctify Myself that they also may be truly sanctified. However, I do not ask only about these but also about those who are believing in Me because of their word, that all may be one, just as You, Father, are in Me and I also in You, that they also may be in Us, so that the world may believe that You sent Me. And the glory You have given Me I have given them that they may be one, just as We are One. I in them and You in Me that they may be perfected into one; that the world may know that You sent Me and God-loved them just as You have God-loved Me. —John 17:19–23

What does it mean to us to understand that God loves His redeemed adopted children just as He loves His only begotten Son? I cannot answer for others, but I will say it changed forever my concept of relationship with God. I understood that Jesus wanted me to enter into a oneness with the Father and with Him. This is no altered state of consciousness achieved with meditation or mind-bending drugs but rather an awareness of being a part of the *Elohim*, the heavenly host of saints and angels, while I am still in the body. And it helps me to understand that I am to God-love as the Father has loved Jesus and me. That is my path—the straight and narrow way.

> "Father God in Heaven, You have loved me just as You loved Jesus. Thank You for saving me and bringing me into oneness with You through Jesus Christ. Help me to love You back and God-love others in the same way as You have loved me so that Your redemption may be known to many others. In the name of Jesus, I pray. Amen."

Monday: Knowing God

How could a person ever know God? How can a temporal mind know the infinite mind of the Almighty? His thoughts are higher than my thoughts. His thinking as far above mine as the sky is above the earth. Of course we believe God knows us because He knows all things, including the desires and motives of our heart.

But how can we know Him in return? It can only be through a relationship with Jesus Christ. Jesus said, "I know My sheep and My sheep hear my voice and follow Me" (John 10:27). We have heard the word of life from the Scripture, and we follow Jesus by faith and His grace saves us. But how can the sheep *know* the Shepherd? Where is the conduit between mortal man and immortal God, between our limited understanding and His all-knowing wisdom? What mechanism can bridge the gap between two dimensions? How can we from the finite perceive the infinite, so that we can know God? I anticipate the reader has thought of the answer already.

> Beloved, let us God-love one another, because God is love. Everyone who God-loves has been born of God and knows God. The one who does not God-love does not know God; for God is love. By this the love of God was shown in us, because God sent His only begotten Son into the world so that we may live through Him. In this is God-love, not that we God-loved Him but that He loved us and sent His Son to be a propitiation for our sins. Beloved, if God so loved us, we are indebted to God-love one another. —1 John 4:7–11

Once more, the key to the knowledge of God and His will for us is in the royal law of Jesus Christ. Obedience to that law is to love God supremely and God-love others sincerely. When we express our God-love for God by submission to His will and obedience to His Word and we do unto others as we would have done to us, we know who God is. We know because we are thinking and acting in a similar way as the Almighty: with God-love.

> "Heavenly Father, thank You for loving me! I hear Your voice through the words of Jesus. I sense Your presence through the Holy Spirit. I know You by God-love, just as the words of the Bible tell me. Help me to God-love others so that I may know them and they may know me. Amen."

Tuesday: Internal Oneness

There is no misery like the agony of the double-minded Christian. I know because I was one. Listening to an angel of conscience on one shoulder and the devil on another reflects a conflict of motives that cannot do anything but bring guilt and sleepless nights. "A double-minded man is unstable in all his ways. ... Come near to God and He will come near to you. Wash clean your hands, sinners, and purify [literally: make holy] your hearts, you double-minded" (James 1:8; 4:8). Yep, that was me, unstable and unable to walk straight on the narrow way. It was not enough to flick the devil off my shoulder. To be single-minded I had to purify and sanctify my heart and let the Holy Spirit fill me with the God-love that only God can give. It is necessary for me to love God with all my heart, soul, mind, and strength so that I might remove the devil *and* the angel of my conscience and listen to the Holy Spirit tell me from the Word of God what I should do. God-love can then motivate me to right action in a single-minded way. The Apostle Paul prayed for the people that they would be guided and motivated to right action by God-love.

> We also have confidence in the Lord, in both what we command you do, and what you indeed will do. Now may the Lord guide your heart straight into the love of God and the endurance of Christ. —2 Thessalonians 3:4–5

We can have confidence in the God-love that has been placed in our heart to guide and motivate us. We do not listen to lies of Satan, and we cannot fully trust our conscience because we all are so skillful in self-justification. Paul prayed the Thessalonians would be guided *straight into* God-love so that they would be unwavering in faith and obedience. God-love never fails. Never.

182

"Lord God, I praise Your name because of Your love and how You God-love me. Make me one with Your God-love; give me single-minded integrity. Guide me straight into Your love and the endurance of Christ. I will not listen to Satan's misleading voice, and I will not fully trust in my own thinking, but I will trust Your Word and God-love to guide me in all things, large and small. Amen."

Wednesday: Nature

The forest seems very still and devoid of life as one walks through. I have found if I stop and sit for a while, preferably in a blind, that after about twenty minutes of sitting quietly and motionless as possible, the forest begins to stir with sound and life. The crows seem to be the first to caw the "all clear" and bring out jays, songbirds, and woodpeckers to resume their symphony. Squirrels begin rustling though dry leaves as a noisy party of distant coyotes celebrates a meal over who knows what. I hear the *put, put, put* of turkeys before I see them. I may spot a deer. The wind picks up a little, and acorns shower down like big raindrops. I feel one with nature. The animals feel I am also, because when I move and my presence becomes known, the animals flee and hide; silence resumes its hold until I leave. I am a fearful part of their world, one with them in creation. The same applies to my domestic animals and pets. I share the world and its fate with them. To love God is to God-love His creation and sense oneness with both. It has been one of my greatest pleasures on the narrow path.

> When I consider Your heavens, the work of Your fingers, the moon and the stars, which You have ordained; what is man that You take thought of him, and the son of man that You care for him? Yet You have made him a little lower than God, and You crown him with glory and majesty! You make him to rule over the works of Your hands; You have put all things under his feet, all sheep and oxen, and also the beasts of the field, the birds of the heavens and the fish of the sea, whatever passes through the paths of the seas. O LORD, our Lord, How majestic is Your name in all the earth! —Psalm 8:3–9 NASB

Some people in the world would want to tell us that we do not belong on this planet; therefore, we exist as intruders in nature. But they do not know the love of God for us or our God-love for Him that makes us one with God and nature.

> "Lord God, You have created me along with every living thing on earth. In my body, I have the plan of life and characteristics that I share with other creatures. I am one with You and nature through Your love. Thank You, Lord. Amen."

Thursday: Unity

There is one thing I have learned about leadership: nothing great can be accomplished by any association, organization, or group unless the people are *united* in purpose and effort behind leadership they trust. If people love the leader, they will join in with leadership and meet any reasonable goal. I have read many books on leadership, and they all emphasize this point: people will try to do the impossible for a leader they love and trust. This applies to families, churches, and government. But saying this and actually building such an *esprit de corps* are two different things and so will guarantee there will always be a new book on leadership.

Talent and charisma by themselves will take a leader no further than a position of leadership. How does a leader get followers to love him or her? I have found an answer in the Book of books by contemplating the life of the greatest leader of the human race—Jesus Christ. He has built the largest and most successful organization the world has ever seen. His true followers love Him and will attempt to do whatever He asks, even at the expense of their lives. How did He get billions of people to love Him like that? He loved them first by going to the Cross. Because of the unity that kind of God-love gives, Jesus could charge His church with a seemingly impossible task.

> Jesus came close to them saying, "All authority has been given me in heaven and on earth. Go make disciples of all nations, baptizing them in the name of the Father, the Son, and the Holy Spirit, teaching them to keep everything I commanded you, and look, I am with you every day until the completion of the age."
> —Matthew 28:18–20

For two thousand years His followers have striven to complete the task. Although Christianity may seem to be fractured by competing human institutions, we are greatly unified in our God-love for Jesus and for our brothers and sisters. Inasmuch as we are unified in the love of Jesus, we have conquered civilizations and baptized hundreds of millions of disciples. Yet we see there remains division and disunity in the body of Christ. If we wish to bring unity to a fractured community, we should imitate our great leader and be the first to show God-love.

> "Lord, help me to be a leader in God-love. Where there is discord, let me bring calmness and peace. When there is division in the fellowship, help me to be the first one to God-love. Help me to show it by what I do. Keep me today on the narrow way of God-love. Amen."

Friday: The Body

I have been a member of the same church for most of the last twenty-five years. Like God, they God-loved me before I ever loved them. They are my family, and I love them with all my heart. We have been through good times and a couple of really rough times. But there is a core of Christians in our fellowship who simply will not give up on each other. We walk together on the narrow path. God-love gives us the unity to survive any trial. Unity has prospered our ministry even when difficulties and trouble threatened the very life of the church.

I had lived in the same community with that church for over twenty years, but I was far from God and unaware of any church that would love me. But when God got hold of my life, I began looking for a fellowship of Christians. My dad was a pastor, so I called him and asked if he could inquire around for some recommendations. He called me back after a couple of days and said a pastor friend knew of a good congregation. I made an appointment with the pastor of the church and told him how I had so much baggage and how my marriage was in a mess and how I felt God wanted me to be a minister and possibly after he got to know me I could teach a Sunday school class or something—and on, and on, and on. He said I should get to know the people, and they should get to know me. Then we would see what could be done. I became one with them and they with me. Ten years later, I knelt with my wife at an altar where I was ordained into ministry. It would have never happened without the oneness with the body of believers that God-love brings.

> Now may the God of endurance and encouragement give to you the same mind in each other according to Christ Jesus. —Romans 15:5

188

The Apostle Paul exhorted the people of Rome to be like Jesus Christ. When we are one with Jesus, we become one with God who gives us endurance and encouragement. We then, in unity and oneness with others on the straight and narrow, give and receive endurance and encouragement. We really do need to be one in the body of Christ.

> "Christ Jesus, I thank You for the endurance and encouragement that You give me. May I be of the same mind toward the church. May I humble myself to receive as well as to give, so that all in the church may be blessed according to the oneness that God-love brings. Amen."

Saturday: In Prayer

There is power in unified prayer by men and women who are one together with their fellowship and with God. When people gather together to pray in common purpose according to the will of God, great things are accomplished. I have seen individual people healed by the grace of God, and I have seen whole congregations healed of division and saved out of destruction when the saints become one in prayer. But I also believe in the power of one godly person who is one with the Father and prays with faith. How much more effective and powerful is prayer when the saints stand together arm in arm to call upon God? And it seems much easier to avoiding stumbling off the straight and narrow when I hang on to others who God-love me as I God-love and hang on to them.

At the end of my dad's ministry, he was a part-time associate at a large church. Years later, the lead pastor at that church told me about how all the pastors prayed at every staff meeting for my dad's hard-case lost son. My mom prayed for me every day from the first she knew that she had conceived. Unified, faithful, and urgent prayer in oneness with God and the saints is very powerful.

> I call upon you, brothers, through our Lord Jesus Christ and through the God-love of the Spirit, to contend together with me in prayers on my behalf, before God, that I may be rescued from those who are disobedient in Jerusalem and that my service may be acceptable to the saints. —Romans 15:30–31

Paul understood the power of prayer and how he, an apostle, needed the support of people who were one with God and unified in prayer. Think of the things that can be accomplished in this way. The people prayed for Paul as he, by the Spirit of God, changed the world! His inspired writing still rules the thinking of much of the world to this very day. That same power is with *us*. But how can Christians be mighty in prayer if we are not one with God and each other? How can we be one if we do not love God supremely and God-love others sincerely?

> "Father in heaven, Your apostle called on the people to pray in oneness with him. Help me to imitate Paul as he has imitated Christ who called on His apostles to pray with Him. May I be one with You and with my brothers and sisters. Amen."

Week 13

The End of the Path

Sunday: Judgment

There is a day coming that will be full of joy for those who truly love God. The day will come unexpectedly, like a thief in the night, surprising the world with total and complete justice. It will be a shock that will compel everyone to confess that Jesus is Lord to the glory of the Father.

Meanwhile, I will confess that it is hard to keep my joy when I think of the injustice of this world. I am offended by those leaders who profess to be concerned about people and yet demonstrate very little of the *actions* that would prove true compassion in them. I ache for our brothers and sisters in this world who are persecuted because they have placed their hope in Jesus. In the last four hundred years, *millions* of Christians have been murdered by those who hate the gospel of Jesus Christ, the twentieth century being the worst. The blood of innocents flows like a river throughout the world. There is little justice for the helpless and weak among us. The thought of these things disturbs my peace and would rob me of joy but for one thing. There is coming a day when Jesus will set everything right. Forever.

> By this God-love has been perfected with us, that we may have confidence in the day of judgment; because as He is, we are also in this world. There is no fear in God-love, but perfect God-love casts out fear, because fear has to do with punishment. The one who does not fear is perfected in God-love. —1 John 4:17–18

It will be a grand and joyful day for those who love God supremely and God-love others sincerely. It will be an awful day for those who do not know or love Him. We who imitate the God-love of Jesus toward the Father and emulate His compassion and mercy

194

toward others have nothing to fear, for we will be saved in the Day of Judgment. We know that God loves us, and grace saves us as we walk the straight and narrow way of God-love. He forgives us when we stumble or wander off the path. His Spirit draws us back with gentleness and great love. What a grand and glorious day will be the day of Christ's return.

> "Father God, thank You for the joy in my heart that Your love has brought to me. Thank you for the confidence I have as I look forward to the great Day of Judgment. Even though I may have tribulation and persecution, I will not fear the future, for I know that You love me. Amen."

Monday: Casuistry Kills

I have a near-infinite capacity for self-justification. I think I must guard against this ability with everything I have. *Casuistry* is the use of subtle reasoning to resolve conflicts in moral laws and rules of ethics. It has been raised to an art form by certain religious societies. Blaise Pascal, a French Christian, mathematician, and philosopher of the seventeenth century, said that the use of casuistry among Christians is simply excuse making. It has fallen into such disrepute that some dictionaries list the synonyms as *self-justification*, *foolishness*, and *sophistry*.

Self-justification is deadly, and I can do it as well as the next person. My employer is not fair in the wage he pays me for my hard work. I deserve to have that which would make my pay more equitable and just; so I justify theft. My spouse is not fulfilling my needs; so I justify adultery. Violent people deserve punishment; so I justify murder. Then I reason, if God has forgiven before, He always will. Therefore I can presume on His grace because I *believe* what I am doing is justified. That is why I fear casuistry. I know I am accountable before the Righteous Judge of the universe and *His* idea of right and wrong. There will be no excuse. What will defeat the casuistry in me? God-love wins every time.

> Moreover, by them [the commandments of God] Your servant is warned; in keeping them there is great reward. Who can discern his errors? Acquit me of hidden faults. Also keep back Your servant from presumptuous sins; let them not rule over me; then I will be blameless, and I shall be acquitted of great transgression. Let the words of my mouth and the meditation of my heart be acceptable in Your sight, O LORD, my rock and my Redeemer. —Psalm 19:11–14 NASB

What is appropriate in the sight of God? Jesus has told us what is acceptable to God. He taught us to love God supremely and God-love others sincerely and produce actions that are the fruit of God-love. If we love Jesus supremely, we will do what He commands. If we God-love others, we will not sin *against* them or *with* them. If we depend on our own justification, there will be no redemption possible as we stand before the bar of God in self-righteousness. *God forbid!*

> "Father in heaven, save me from self-righteousness. I am justified by Your grace. But I know by Your Word that I will have to give an account for the deeds I have done in my life, whether good or evil. Help me, God, that my actions may spring from God-love and not my own justification of evil desires and temptations. May Your grace be upon me. Amen."

Tuesday: The End of the Age

I am contemplating the fate of the universe as I write this. I am sitting in a booth at an internet café nursing a cup of coffee while being taught that all things are coming to an end. The paper cup of coffee on the table is growing cold as I pause occasionally from the keyboard to sip. Every once in a while, I have to take it to the microwave to infuse some more energy into the brew. The liquid continually suffers heat loss. It demonstrates the second law of thermodynamics, which tells us that the entire universe is suffering energy decay and will eventually (billions of years from now) suffer the same fate as my coffee and become a burned-out cinder ever expanding into darkness.

God created this reality in which He placed us and every other living thing. Space and time are the Lord's and they have a beginning and an end according to His will. But the end has more to do with God's love for us and our God-love for Him than the second law of thermodynamics. My bathroom mirror teaches me that my body is suffering inevitable decay and that the end of my existence in this reality will probably occur well before the second coming of Jesus Christ and certainly before the end of the natural world. At the beginning of the narrow path laid out for me is a gate—Jesus Christ is the name of it. At the end of the straight and narrow path is my death, what John Bunyan described in *The Pilgrim's Progress* as crossing a river of uncertain depth. God-love will keep me on the path to the very end. His grace and mercy will justify me beyond the river.

> Inasmuch as it is fated for people once to die and afterwards the judgment, so also Christ, having been offered up once to carry away the sins of many, will be seen a second time without blood to those who are eagerly expecting Him for salvation. —Hebrews 9:27–28

It is difficult for us to think about our own death. We must not be morbid, but we must be prepared by grace and good deeds along the narrow path to meet the God who loves us with everlasting God-love. The reason we received Christ is that we may have eternal life, beginning in this present reality. Because God loves us and we God-love Him, we have confidence in our life to come.

> "Father in heaven, 'Even though I walk through the valley of the shadow of death, I will fear no evil,' because You love me and have filled me with Your Spirit. Help me walk the narrow path with God-love to the end of my life. Amen."

Wednesday: Ever-Ready

There is no human knowledge that will inform me of the time of the end of the straight and narrow path that I must walk. The time of my demise is *uncertain,* and I cannot see it. What is certain is that it *will* come. I have lived a long time already and soon will be beyond average life expectancy. Every birthday brings the end of the path closer. I do not think of it often, but when I do, I remember that Jesus loves me, and I love Him. That gives me faith that the path will end well.

There is a lot of curiosity among Christians about the time at the end of the age when *everyone's* path will end. Even the apostles asked Jesus about the end of the age and when that would come. Jesus gave them some signs of the end, but his exhortation to them was to be *awake, alert,* and *ready,* because no one knows the day or the hour of His return when He will bring the age to an end.

> Be awake and alert, for you do not know the day on which your Lord comes. And you know that if the master of the house had known in which watch the thief was coming, he would have stayed awake and alert and not have allowed the thief to dig through the wall of his house. For this reason, you also must be ready. For the Son of Man comes in the hour you do not suppose he will. —Matthew 24:42–44

When He spoke this somber warning in Matthew 24 and 25, Jesus also gave seven illustrations and parables about being ready. They are the fig tree, the days of Noah, the thief in the night, the just and unjust servants, the ten virgins, the talents, and the sheep and the goats. All of these parables have to do either with our relationship to God or our relationship to others.

Whether it is the end of the age or our personal end, the key to being in right relationship is to walk the straight and narrow in obedience to the command of Jesus to love God supremely and God-love others sincerely. Our journey on the narrow path begins in God-love, continues in God-love, and ends successfully in God-love. So be ever ready in God-love, and do not worry about the time of the end of the straight and narrow.

> "Lord Jesus, thank You for the warning that I receive from Your words. Help me, Lord, to be ever-ready in God-love by being obedient to Your commands and doing unto others as I would have done unto me. I know You will be with me all the way. Amen."

Thursday: Heaven and the Other Place

He was one of the best-behaved children I have ever seen. I was at a camp meeting sponsored by my church. I was enjoying the music and singing by the couple that was leading worship in a large tabernacle. While the man and woman led on the platform, their toddler son sat in a stroller at the end of the front row. He amused himself with a toy and sat quietly even though they left him unattended. I commented to his mother that I was amazed by the good behavior of their son. She replied, "Yes, he is well-behaved, because if he acts up, I will send him to the nursery. He hates the nursery, and all I have to do is mouth the word, 'nursery,' from the platform, and he settles right down." The boy had never been in the nursery in that building and did not even know where it was. But he knew the nursery was real, the nursery was *really* bad, and he *really* did not want to go to the nursery.

I do not know where hell is, but I know it is a *real* place. Jesus taught often of it, speaking of never-ending darkness and fire, eternal punishment without death. Hell is *really bad,* and I *really* do not want to go there. But I have confidence in the grace of God in Jesus Christ. I love God with all of my heart and try to God-love others as the Holy Spirit helps me on the narrow way. As I walk along, I try to imagine heaven, my future home.

> But just as it has been written, "Things which eye did not see, and ear did not hear, and did not arise in the heart of man, are the things God has prepared for those who are God-loving Him." —1 Corinthians 2:9

We have no worries about eternal punishment when we walk the narrow path with love for God and others. God knows those who love Him with genuine God-love. He has prepared a wonderful place for us, and His grace is the title to our eternal home.

> "God, I am so thankful for Your grace and mercy toward me. I know I will be in heaven with You because You love me, and I love You. You have placed Your Spirit in my heart and brought me Your love. Day by day You transform my life and teach me the ways of God-love. I owe everything to You. I pray that You would help me today to God-love others and save me from hypocrisy. In the name of Jesus, I pray. Amen."

Friday: Questions and Answers

Whether one believes in God or not, life is full of unanswered questions. If I am honest with God, I will confide every doubt and difficult question to Him. He never seems to find fault in that. There seem to be more questions at the beginning of the straight and narrow than toward the end. But many remain, and these are settled in my mind by faith and the knowledge that God loves me with everlasting God-love.

The ontological questions about creation and the existence of God are settled to my satisfaction by the host of unanswerable questions that dog the atheists. The heavens actually *do* declare the glory of God, and the sky proclaims the work of His hands (Psalm 19:1–6).

The harder questions, to me, begin with *why* and *how long*? The definitive answers to most of these questions must wait until the end of the path when I will discover the whole truth and discern the thoughts of God. Many of the saints in the Bible asked those questions. Moses, Job, Jeremiah, and Habakkuk are among those who asked the why and how long questions. From the Cross, Jesus asked the most poignant.

> The sixth hour came, and it became dark over the earth until the ninth hour. And at the ninth hour Jesus shouted out in a loud voice, "Eloi, Eloi, lama sabachthani?" which is interpreted, "My God, My God, why did You forsake Me?" —Mark 15:33–34

Even our Lord had the why question. His answer came in the resurrection, at the end of His path among us. We can look at that and have confidence that all our questions will be answered at the end of the path. But in the moment on the path when life delivers a cruel and awful blow, knowing we will have an answer "someday" is not enough. That is when we need to let ourselves be enfolded in the love of God and have faith that He will somehow bring comfort to our hurting heart. We press onward with that knowledge and our God-love toward Him.

> "Father in heaven, I do not have answers for myself or others when they ask why and how long. I only know You love me, and You love them. Comfort me in the Holy Spirit. Be with my brothers and sisters in their unanswered questions. Help me to love them and comfort them. Keep me from platitudes and empty words. Amen."

Saturday: The One Who Is

It is for the end of the path that I made a beginning through the small gate. I want to *live*. I can see no hope in the noble words or redemptive efforts of men. Only in a faith-grace-love relationship with Jesus Christ will I have immortality. I am amused but saddened by the people who spend their fortunes to be cryogenically preserved after their death in the hopes that future science will give them back their life. Compassion for them wells up in me for I know and understand their desire for immortality. The Word says, "In Him (Jesus) was life, and the life was the light of men" (John 1:4). The Greek word translated "life" in this verse is *zōē*, meaning physical life. From this word we name our *zoos*. Jesus and His blood, which washed away my sins, is the gate at the beginning. That same grace will be with me at the end of my life when the narrow way of God-love ends for me. He is not called the Alpha and Omega, the First and the Last, for nothing.

> To the One who God-loves us and has loosed us from our sins by His blood and has made us a kingdom, priests unto God His Father, to Him be the glory and the power into the age of the ages. ... "I Am the Alpha and Omega," says the Lord God, "the One who is, the One who was, the One who is coming, the Omnipotent." —Revelation 1:6, 8

When he was commissioned by God to begin a seemingly impossible mission, Moses shrank back in fear and self-doubt. God assured him that He would always be with him. Moses was not so sure and asked the One who spoke from the burning bush, "When people ask me, 'What is the name of the one who sent you?' what shall I tell them?" (Exodus 3:13). The Greek translation of the Old Testament, which the Apostles used, has the same words in Exodus for the name of God that John the Revelator gives in Revelation, "Egō eimi ho ōn; I am the One who is" (Revelation 1:8). Does anyone doubt that God was with Moses to the end of his path? God even took the body of Moses away from the people and buried Moses Himself. Likewise, God tells us that in Jesus Christ He is always with us from the first moment we start our journey on the straight and narrow to the last breath we take on the path of God-love. He will see to our final glorious, victorious end in this life. Love God supremely and God-love others sincerely on the way that leads to eternal life.

> "Lord God, thank You for life. Thank You for coming into this world to live among us, to show Your God-love by suffering as humanity suffers. No, You suffered *more* than we suffer. Thank You for Your grace that brings eternal life. I pray that the words of this devotional will bring glory to Your name because of the God-love people will show to You by their obedience and good works. I know You are with me all the way. In the name of Jesus, I pray. Amen."

Bibliography

Aland, B., K. Aland, J. Karividopoulos, C. M. Martini, and B. M. Metzger, eds. *The Greek New Testament.* Stuttgart, Germany: Deutsche Bibelgesellschaft, 1993.

Brenton, L. C. L. *The Septuagint with Apocrypha: Greek and English.* 10th printing. Peabody, Massachusetts: Hendrickson Publishers, 2003.

Gotchius, E. V. N. *The Language of the New Testament.* New York, NY: Charles Scribner's Sons, 1965.

Mounce, W. D. *The Analytical Lexicon to the Greek New Testament.* Grand Rapids, MI: Zondervan Publishing House, 1993.

Strong, James. *Strong's Concordance.* Austin, TX: WORD*search*, 2007. WORD*search* CROSS e-book.

von Tischendorf, Constantin. *Tischendorf Interlinear Bible— Tischendorf Interlinear New Testament.* Austin, TX: WORD*search* Corp., 2009. WORD*search* CROSS e-book.

Zodhiates, S. *The Complete Word Study Dictionary: New Testament.* Chattanooga, TN: AMG Publishers, 1992.

If you enjoyed this book, will you consider sharing the message with others?

Let us know your thoughts at info@newhopepublishers.com. You can also let the author know by visiting or sharing a photo of the cover on our social media pages or leaving a review at a retailer's site. All of it helps us get the message out!

Twitter.com/NewHopeBooks

Facebook.com/NewHopePublishers

Instagram.com/NewHopePublishers

New Hope® Publishers, Ascender Books, Iron Stream Books, and New Hope Kidz are imprints of Iron Stream Media, which derives its name from Proverbs 27:17, "As iron sharpens iron, so one person sharpens another."

This sharpening describes the process of discipleship, one to another. With this in mind, Iron Stream Media provides a variety of solutions for churches, ministry leaders, and nonprofits ranging from in-depth Bible study curriculum and Christian book publishing to custom publishing and consultative services. Through the popular Life Bible Study and Student Life Bible Study brands, ISM provides web-based full-year and short-term Bible study teaching plans as well as printed devotionals, Bibles, and discipleship curriculum.

For more information on ISM and
New Hope Publishers, please visit

IronStreamMedia.com

NewHopePublishers.com